MW00836860

CALL ME CRAZY

To Peggy,
Keep it up!!!

[signature]

CALL ME CRAZY

Stories from the Mad Movement

IRIT SHIMRAT

PRESS GANG PUBLISHERS
VANCOUVER

Copyright © 1997 Irit Shimrat

1   2   3   4   00   99   98   97

All rights reserved. This book may not be reproduced in part or in whole by any means
without written permission from the Publisher, except for the use of short passages for review
purposes. All correspondence should be addressed to Press Gang Publishers.

The Publisher acknowledges financial assistance from the Book Publishing Industry
Development Program of the Department of Canadian Heritage, the Cultural Services
Branch, Province of British Columbia, and from The Canada Council for the Arts.

Canadian Cataloguing in Publication Data

Shimrat, Irit, 1958–
Call me crazy

Includes bibliographical references.
ISBN 0-88974-070-4

1. Shimrat, Irit, 1958– —Health.   2. Ex-mental patients—Biography.   3. Antipsychiatry.
4. Psychiatry—Political aspects.   5. Alternatives to psychiatric hospitalization.   I. Title.
RC464.S54A3   1997   616.89'0092   C97-910059-3

Editing by Barbara Kuhne
Cover and text designed by Val Speidel
Author photograph by Elaine Ayers
Typeset in Berkeley Oldstyle and Goudy Sans
Printed by Best Book Manufacturers
Printed and bound in Canada

Press Gang Publishers
225 East 17th Avenue, Suite 101
Vancouver, B.C. V5V 1A6 Canada
Tel: 604-876-7787 Fax: 604-876-7892

ACKNOWLEDGEMENTS

I thank:

Persimmon Blackbridge, for making an impossible task easy;

Chris Bearchell, Will Pritchard and Andrew Sorfleet for emergency writing help above and beyond the call of duty;

Michael Weyman, for superb last-minute proofing;

Geoffrey Reaume, for his annotated reading list (" 'Madness,' Medicine and Mythology");

The members of Support Coalition International for their quick responses to my e-mail request for bibliographic help;

Larry Halff, for his support and the use of his laser printer (and all the paper);

Barbara Kuhne and Della McCreary of Press Gang Publishers: Barb for her patience, wisdom and superb editing skills; and Della for her tireless efforts in letting the world know this book exists;

Catherine Bennett, for a thorough and thoughtful copy editing job;

Val Speidel, for the cover and book design;

The people of a certain magical island, which will remain unnamed (you know who you are), for all the fun and music;

My mother, for loving me even though I go on and on about psychiatry;

And last, but certainly not least, the Explorations Program of the Canada Council, for the loot!

This book is dedicated to the people I interviewed for it and to everyone else in the mad movement—heroes, one and all.

CONTENTS

PART TWO: ONTARIO PSYCHIATRIC SURVIVORS' ALLIANCE

PART THREE: MIGHTY MADWOMEN

PART FOUR: HOPE

INTRODUCTION

Call Me Crazy is about people who have done an unusual thing: we stopped being mental patients. That's not supposed to happen, since mental illness is supposed to be an incurable biological disease. Certainly you're not supposed to reject the idea that you're sick, stop taking your medications, refuse to ever see a psychiatrist again, join with others in questioning psychiatry and get a life as a result. That would mean they were wrong about you. That might mean they're wrong about a lot of people.

The concept of mental illness is a powerful and useful one. It generates a great deal of money not only for drug companies but also for psychiatrists, psychologists, therapists, social workers, mental health bureaucrats, hospital staff and community mental health workers. It also deters people from taking a hard look at what's really gone wrong in the lives of those who are in emotional trouble.

If you can't function or don't want to go on living or are overwhelmed by terror, rage or any strong emotion, what our society has to offer—and what we've been taught to believe will help—is psychiatry. But are unacceptable feelings and behaviour really caused by a disease of the brain, on which psychiatrists are the experts? Are the treatments they give people really alleviating symptoms? Not even psychiatrists themselves claim to be able to cure anyone of mental illness. Could it be that something else is going on?

Psychiatric treatment seeks to help (or make) people conform to social norms. It aims to produce successful, productive people who can function and fit in. But what if success, productivity and "normal" functioning can sometimes be achieved only at the expense of creativity and critical thinking? What if social norms need to change in order for the world to become a better place? What if change is better than stagnation, and nonconforming people are an important source of change?

Many people who go (or are put) into a mental hospital or psychiatric ward get diagnosed and drugged and become mental patients for life. It is no longer nearly as common as it used to be to keep people in for years at a time, though there are people in provincial hospitals who have been there for decades and are expected to die there. But once you're diagnosed, you're generally told you have to stay on drugs forever. You are expected to (and therefore expect to, and therefore often do) fall apart whenever anything in your life goes wrong; require continuous professional help; and go back into the hospital now and again when things get really bad. You are likely to see a therapist, counsellor, psychologist or psychiatrist on a regular basis, which reinforces the idea that you are sick and need help. If you are deemed severely mentally ill, you may well be told that you can never work again, and be given an inadequate lifelong pension and put in some kind of supportive housing facility.

All of the people whose stories are told in this book are part of a loosely defined social movement (international in scope, very small in Canada) whose members believe that this kind of thing is not good for people and not necessary. Many of us believe that there's no such thing as mental illness; that what goes wrong when people go crazy or become unbearably unhappy has to do with how people live and what happens to them, rather than chemical imbalances in their brains. Our movement has many names and many aspects. It has been called the mental patients' liberation movement, the antipsychiatry movement, the psychiatric survivors' movement (psychiatric survivors are people who consider themselves to have survived, rather than benefited from, psychiatric treatment), the c/s/x movement (Consumer/Survivor/eX-patient). There will be more about language later; in the interests of simplicity, I've used the term "mad movement" in this book.

People in the mad movement, like people in any social movement, argue a lot. But most of us tend to agree on certain basic principles; for example, that electroshock and forcible drugging are not acceptable practices. Groups and individuals have found strength in coming together and sharing information, and have done important work. People I interviewed for this book have battled the mental health and social service systems in defence of their own and others' rights, sometimes successfully. These people's experiences have led them to think about how people in emotional trouble could get better help than that available within the system. Some have created plays, music, films, videos, radio and television shows, books, paintings, magazines, newsletters and computer information networks. Some have provided alternatives to psychiatric treatment. All have strong ideas about why the mad movement is necessary:

"When you're locked up you're treated like a prisoner, even though you haven't committed a crime. You're deprived of your liberty without due process. But, unlike a prisoner, you don't know when, or whether, you're going to get out."

"They use force on us in hospital. They don't recognize the connection between abuse and emotional problems."

"Why should we be in hospital if there's nothing physically wrong with us? What do emotions and behaviour have to do with doctors or hospitals?"

"No one investigates the fraudulent claims of researchers who say they've found the gene for schizophrenia. Whoever pays for the study ends up with the results they want."

"In the mental health system you're never asked what you have to offer. Sometimes you're so drugged you don't know what you can offer. The focus is entirely on what's supposed to be wrong with you."

"It's like the system is trying to turn everybody into vanilla, and maybe when you went in, you were chocolate almond swirl."

About psychiatry

Psychiatrists and their predecessors—the "mad-doctors" and alienists—have been doing things to patients' bodies in the attempt to heal their minds for hundreds of years. Most people assume that the methods now used are legitimate and scientific, and that a lot of progress has been made with the passage of time. True, psychiatrists no longer rip out people's internal organs to cure them of mental illness, as Henry A. Cotton did at Trenton State Hospital in New Jersey, where he was superintendent from 1907 to 1933 (Collins, 1988). Insulin shock treatment—giving someone enough insulin to induce a coma—became unpopular in the 1960s. The "cold wet pack" (wrap patient tightly in sheets, then lower into ice-cold water and steep several hours, adding ice as necessary) has not been used in North America since the 1980s, as far as I know. Lobotomy—gouging out bits of people's brains with sharp objects—is considerably less common than it used to be, though I know of a man who had the more modern kind of lobotomy—done with a laser beam—in Toronto in 1989. He was assured it would cure his depression. A few months later he killed himself.

Diagnoses are supposed to be more scientific now too. For example, homosexuality is no longer deemed an illness requiring psychiatric treatment, though it was until 1973. However, now we have such diseases as "anorexia nervosa," which in lay terms means being too well socialized as a woman, and whose symptoms consist of trying to make oneself vanish. And there are still the old standbys like "personality disorder." More than one person with this label has come to the conclusion that it means the psychiatrist really, really doesn't like the person he or she is diagnosing.

The fact is that virtually every human emotion, every kind of behaviour and every way of perceiving things can be found listed under one disease or another in the *Diagnostic and Statistical Manual*—psychiatry's disease bible.

A famous Canadian psychiatrist

D. Ewen Cameron founded Montreal's Allen Memorial Institute in 1944 and went on to become one of Canada's most influential and highly placed psychiatrists. In 1961, he organized the World Congress of Psychiatry, which led to the founding of the World Psychiatric Association. He was the first president of both the Canadian and American Psychiatric Associations.

At the Allen Memorial Institute, in the 1950s and 1960s, Cameron combined "sleep therapy" (knocking people out for days and sometimes weeks at a time), various dubious drugs and huge numbers of electroshock treatments to "depattern" his patients. In other words, he would clean up the dysfunctioning mind until there was just about nothing left in there, so that he could then put the right stuff in. This was done by means of Cameron's brainchild, "psychic driving": the patient had to listen to up to sixteen hours a day of taped repetitions of what Cameron considered instructive statements. Cameron boasted of a successful case: "He lives in the immediate present. All schizophrenic symptoms have disappeared. There is complete amnesia for all events of his life." Many of Cameron's "patients" had to be fed and diapered toward the end of their treatment (Collins, *op. cit.*).

D. Ewen Cameron no doubt felt that he was doing his best to help the less fortunate. However, his research was funded by the CIA as part of MK-Ultra, a covert study of brainwashing techniques in which the Canadian government cooperated. His severely damaged "patients"—those who were able—had a long hard fight to get the government to admit that this had ever happened. With help from the Canadian mad movement, some of them finally succeeded in bringing this matter to court many years after Cameron's death, and were awarded too little money, much too late.

Cameron's experiments are over. But aspects of his mindset still prevail among psychiatrists today. One such premise is that any treatment, no matter how brutal or ineffective, is justifiable when used on people who are seen as hopeless.

Psychiatric drugs and other treatments

One of the most popular ways of dealing with crazy people today is the use of a class of drugs known as neuroleptics (also called phenothiazines, major tranquillizers or antipsychotics). *Taber's Cyclopedic Medical Dictionary* defines neuroleptic drugs as "medicines which produce symptoms resembling those of diseases of the nervous system" (Tenenbein 1995). Sudden death is listed as a possible adverse effect of these drugs, usually caused by the drugs' interference with the gag reflex: people die from breathing vomit into their lungs and suffocating on it.

One of the most common effects of long-term use of neuroleptics is a disfiguring and sometimes debilitating neurological disease called tardive dyskinesia. Neuroleptics can also cause stiffness, restlessness, insomnia, drowsiness, constipation, confusion, lack of muscle coordination, anxiety, agitation, depression, weakness, fever, headache, spasms, heart problems, immune system problems, liver disease, urinary problems, nausea, vomiting, diarrhea, impotence, bone marrow poisoning and convulsions. Their use can result in exacerbation of psychosis—you get crazier from the drugs—and withdrawal psychosis is quite common if you suddenly stop using them (which of course is interpreted as meaning that your illness is returning, and you need to get right back on the drugs). And they are given together with other drugs meant to counteract the adverse effects, which cause adverse effects of their own.

Neuroleptics can produce a condition called neuroleptic malignant syndrome, which can be fatal. This is an extreme toxic reaction occurring in a small number of people who take these drugs. It closely resembles a disease caused lethargic encephalitis, characterized by fever, sweating, unstable cardiovascular signs and in severe cases coma and death. Finally, people who take neuroleptics are very sensitive to heat; some have died during heat waves.

Other popular psychiatric drugs are lithium, antidepressants and minor tranquillizers. Lithium is prescribed for manic depression (bipolar affective disorder, or BAD). The "therapeutic" level is close to the toxic one, so frequent blood tests are necessary. Lithium can cause nausea, vomiting, diarrhea, tremors, weight gain, impotence, kidney disease, urinary problems, dizziness, weakness, liver problems, muscle spasms, hallucinations, delirium, confusion and seizures.

Antidepressants can cause nausea, drowsiness, weakness, constipation, insomnia, tremors, anxiety, delirium, hostility, menstrual problems, impotence, liver and heart problems, weight gain, seizures and stroke.

Minor tranquillizers (such as Valium and Rivotril) are prescribed for anxiety. They can cause dizziness, slurred speech, seizures, weakness, fainting, headache, confusion, memory problems, hallucinations, depression, nausea, weight gain, fever, constipation, diarrhea, menstrual and sexual problems, sensitivity to light, blurred vision, excitement, agitation and anger. They are extremely addictive and withdrawal problems can be severe.

If the drugs don't produce the desired effect (and they often don't), the dose is likely to be increased, or a similar drug tried. If that doesn't work, frequently the next step is the use of "chemical cocktails"—combinations of psychiatric drugs, within the same class of drugs and/or across classes. I know of many cases where drugs have been combined that the standard reference texts say should not be prescribed together. In some of these cases the results were lethal.

If you persistently fail to "respond" to drug treatment, you may end up getting electroshock (ECT): an electric current is passed through your brain, inducing a convulsion that is somehow supposed to make you better. The people who give ECT say they don't know how it works; it just does. Its critics say that it "works" by causing brain damage: people may feel better for a while as a result of euphoria like that sometimes caused by other kinds of head injuries. And, like other head injuries, ECT causes confusion, disorientation and memory loss, often permanent. Certainly one is less bothered by problems one can no longer remember or concentrate on. But I have met people who, as the result of ECT, have lost years of their lives; who have had to learn all over again not only how to read and write but also how to recognize their own families; who have lost the skills and abilities that they felt had made them who they were.

Why is the use of shock and drug treatments so widespread if it causes so much damage? Besides being lucrative (psychiatrists make a hefty fee each time they push the button on the shock machine, and the huge profits generated by the pharmaceutical industry are well known), it makes the inmates of psychiatric institutions and wards far easier to control. It also saves mental health professionals from having to think very much about how to help people, or even about the fact that people are different from each other: whatever the problem, they can just write a prescription. The relatives, lovers, roommates and friends of crazy people, who often experience enormous stress and have no idea how to help, can hand the problem over to experts. And of course the treatments promise relief from suffering to the people whom this is all about: the people psychiatry labels mentally ill, whose lives are often devastated by strange experiences they can't understand or control.

Some people have told me that psychiatric treatment works for them. I believe them. All kinds of things can help someone who desperately wants to be helped, especially if that person trusts those doing the helping. It's my observation that different drugs have different effects on different people at different times. What a mood-altering drug, prescribed or otherwise, will do for you—or to you—depends on many variables besides biochemistry. For example, it matters a lot what you *think* it will do.

But what if biochemical imbalances and genetic defects are not actually the root of the problem? Yes, some people go mad and become disconnected from or uninterested in their usual realities. Yes, some people become so unhappy they can't cope with life. And it's a safe bet that when these things happen, brain chemistry is affected, just as it is when you're frightened, angry or in love. But saying such changes are caused by the chemical imbalances is like saying that fear is caused by adrenaline.

What if the price people pay for relief—those who do find relief at the hands of psychiatry—not only is too high, but also doesn't make any sense? What if there are a hundred other things that would work as well or better, and which don't pose the risk of adverse effects?

Over the years, quite a few people have believed that this was the case, including psychiatrists Thomas Szasz, R. D. Laing and Peter Breggin. All three, and others, have written extensively about the idea, first formulated by Szasz (as far as I know), that "mental illness" is a metaphor that has been acted upon as if it were a scientific reality, to people's detriment. But very few people know their work, relative to the millions persuaded otherwise by the media, agencies like the Canadian Mental Health Association, and groups like the Schizophrenia Society (formerly Friends of Schizophrenics) or, in the U.S., the National Alliance for the Mentally Ill (NAMI). It should be noted that these organizations, like professional psychiatric associations, get their "educational" materials directly from drug companies.

Psychiatric treatment is not just a matter of drugs and electroshock. From the patient's viewpoint, it also involves learning to believe that you're damaged goods, less than other people, defective. That you're not okay, and you'll never be okay, but you can be more like other people. To get there, though, you may need all kinds of treatment. If you're not compliant—and being compliant doesn't always occur to you when you're crazy and terrified—the treatment includes putting you in "seclusion" (solitary confinement) and shackling you to a bed.

Once you're diagnosed, they've really got you. Laugh too much, cry too much, talk too much, don't talk enough—or, god forbid, get angry—and the people around you think you're getting "sick" again. And how likely are you to be believed about anything? Some people get beaten and raped in hospital, sometimes by staff. But if they complain about it, they may well be told they were hallucinating.

As a mental patient, you don't just lose your credibility with other people; you're taught not to believe in or trust *yourself*. You're taught to doubt your own perceptions: they may be signs of your illness. It's especially bad if you don't think you're sick. That means you have no "insight"—the psychiatric term for agreeing with your doctor about what's wrong with you and what should be done about it. If you fail to appreciate the nature of your illness, you will be deemed incompetent to make treatment decisions. As the process of declaring you mentally incompetent, or incapable—carried out by psychiatrists, of course—allows other people to legally make decisions on your behalf, lack of insight can be grounds for drugging you against your will.

I believe that the "science" of psychiatry is arcane, bizarre and hurtful. While you're reading this, people all over this country are being locked up, tied down and injected with dangerous drugs. Even more people are attending programs at clinics and centres where they're being taught that they're not okay. Such "treatment" has got to stop.

About this book

I went crazy in 1978 and again in 1979, and was locked up in a total of three psychiatric facilities, ending in 1980. In 1986 I became editor of *Phoenix Rising: The Voice of the Psychiatrized*, an internationally distributed magazine founded by mad movement activists Don Weitz and Carla McKague. In 1990 I helped found the Ontario Psychiatric Survivors' Alliance (OPSA), a coalition of political action and self-help groups run by and for people who had been through the mental health system. I coordinated OPSA until 1992.

In this book, I tell how I came to the mad movement and what I saw and did there. My story is interspersed with those of some of the most interesting and thoughtful people I've met along the way. I interviewed people in the Yukon, British Columbia, Ontario and Quebec, mostly in late 1994. Lanny Beckman was interviewed in 1995, and Jennifer Chambers revised her interview in 1996. Other updates, as well as my interjected comments, appear in square brackets.

Almost everyone I interviewed has been diagnosed mentally ill. The few who have not have nevertheless dedicated their professional lives to fighting against such labelling and the damage that stems from it.

I quote a lot of people. Only those quoted at length are named. Generally, series of quotations that are not attributed to anyone come from group discussions that I tape-recorded and then transcribed. I could have summarized what people had to say, but I've chosen to let them say it for themselves. They say it better than I could.

Part One of *Call Me Crazy* tells the story of me going nuts, getting locked up, getting out and getting active, as well as the stories of some of the activists who began the Canadian movement. Part Two focusses on the Ontario Psychiatric Survivors' Alliance, which was one of the most visible manifestations of the movement. Part Three contains the stories of five women who have had psychiatric treatment and who have gone on to do work that has improved the quality of their own and many other people's lives. Part Four takes a look at alternatives to psychiatry. Finally, there is a bibliography that I hope will be useful to people wanting to know more.

ONE

CRAZY

O

All my life, people have been telling me I'm weird.

As a child, I was fairly happy. I was not abused. I was a good student and liked school. I guess that's pretty weird. As a suburban teenager, I did the kinds of things my friends did: experimented with drugs and sex, got into music. I liked reading, writing, drawing, listening to a.m. radio and watching *The Monkeys* and *The Avengers* on TV. I wrote stories and told jokes that my friends found strange. But to me, I seemed like a normal kid.

I was shy as a child, like many little girls. But getting into the drama club in high school changed that. In my final year, I got the lead in a play in the Simpson's Drama Festival, which was a big deal. My character in the play went nuts and got locked up. It was fun pretending to be crazy and acting melodramatic.

Meanwhile, though, I'd started having boyfriends. They were nice boys, but the girlfriend role bothered me and I ended up feeling resentful. Then I'd feel guilty about feeling resentful. I worried a lot about being a bad person. I started to hit myself and yank at my hair, hard, when no one was looking.

I finished my first year of university in 1979. I'd fallen in love with John, a boy I'd met in French class. John was tall and sensitive and had beautiful, long, curly hair. He told me he was an anarchist and a feminist. I thought he was wonderful. But then he went to Spain for the summer, and I was bitterly unhappy.

September finally arrived. John came home, only to tell me he was crazy about this woman he'd met in Spain, and hoped he and I could just be friends. Around the same time, my father announced that he was getting married again and I couldn't live with him anymore. A few days later, school started, and I found out I had not been accepted into the creative writing program. This was perhaps the most terrible shock of all. Everyone had always told me I was a good writer, and I'd believed it.

However, I discovered that I didn't have to worry about any of this, because the planet I'd thought I was living on had suddenly become something entirely different. I realized I was embroiled in a huge conflict that had to do with saving the world. There were good people and bad people. Fortunately, I could tell who was who just by looking. I was definitely one of the good guys. My worries about my own badness miraculously vanished.

I was delighted to discover, on my very first day of classes, that my teachers were all psychic; every single one of them could read my mind. But, unless I wore sunglasses, I couldn't look them or anyone else in the eye, because the intensity of my gaze could kill. So I always wore sunglasses. I'd go into the store downstairs in the Ross Building at York University (the building where my father, a math professor, had his office), scoop up sunglasses by the handful and walk out with them, knowing I was invisible. Sitting in class, I'd put on a new pair of sunglasses every few minutes.

My diet consisted entirely of a pint carton of milk a day. I'd walk into the store, take a carton and walk out drinking it, secure in the knowledge that no one could see me. God spoke to me through my alarm clock when I held it up to my ear. God was the collective unconsciousness of women. Its voice was soft and sweet. Alas, I can't remember anything it said.

In the library, I borrowed a pen from a stranger and wrote on the wall,

"Rejoice, brothers and sisters. God is dead. He died in 1949 squared, in Manchester, England-England, in the body of Albert Einstein."

It came to me that I was in love with my English teacher. I went to his office to tell him. The door was locked. I put my hand on the doorknob and concentrated really hard. I turned it, and walked in. I sat at his desk, waiting for him, doodling on a piece of scrap paper. After a while he came in. He was very upset, and he asked how I got in there. I told him I opened the door. He said it was locked. "I know," I said, "but I opened it." Then I put my arms around him and told him I loved him. He disengaged as fast as he could and strongly suggested I get psychiatric help. I left.

I heard the music of the universe playing down on the first floor of the Ross Building. I followed my ears until I found an all-women band, playing keyboard, drums, bass and guitar. I boldly approached the keyboard player and said, "If you play just a little slower, it will be perfect." She did. It was.

Then the band was gone, and there were people sitting in a ring of chairs, with me in the middle. I circled slowly, taking the hand of each of them in my hands and saying, "I'm your mother, and you don't have to worry about anything. Everything's going to be okay."

Then I was talking with this boy who told me his name was David Miller. He wore glasses, and so did I. He said he had astigmatism in his left eye, and I said, "That's amazing! I have astigmatism in my right eye!" (Apart from not really being amazing, this wasn't even true.) I invited him into my father's office and kissed him. He was afraid my father would come in, but I told him that was impossible. We agreed to meet in the cafeteria for coffee the next day, and he left. A moment later my father arrived, ready to drive me home. In the car I told him I could make the traffic lights green all the way. He looked at me strangely. The traffic lights were green all the way.

That night, I broke my glasses (my prescription ones, not the stolen sunglasses) in half, on purpose. I explained to my father that my vision was not "bad," as I'd been told. It was just different. My father was very, very frightened to find that his witty, intellectual daughter had gone out of her mind. He had no idea what to do with me, so he took me to our family doctor the next day.

I never did get to meet David Miller for coffee. The doctor talked to me for a few minutes and advised me to sign myself into the psychiatric ward at the local hospital. Eager for any kind of guidance, I did what he said.

The next thing I knew, somebody was coming at me with a needle. When I resisted, several people grabbed me. Gazing up at all these angry strangers, I saw that one of them was a huge, handsome black man with one blue and one brown eye. I realized he was half angel and half devil. I stared into his brown eye, which was the angel eye. While they were stripping me and rolling me over and shooting me up in the ass, I focussed my energy on reaching his soul, begging him not to let them hurt me.

They put me on a stretcher and rolled me into a little, featureless room. There was a door with a window in it, a bare mattress and nothing else. There were straps running under the mattress, and I was trussed up on it, shackled at the wrists and ankles.

Terror.

Why won't they tell me what game this is and what the rules are? Is there anybody else on my side? Are they going to kill me?

I yelled and screamed and chanted magic words I was sure would get me out of there. It didn't work. I tried to twist my body into weird positions: if I came up with exactly the right combination of contorted limbs, they would let me go. It didn't work.

People came in every now and again to feed me or give me another shot. But when I yelled and yelled that I had to go to the bathroom, they ignored me. I decided they must want me to dirty the floor and totally humiliate myself. Then they'd be happy and set me free. It didn't work.

Time passed, very slowly. One day, they removed my shackles. I discovered a soft grey rubber button on the wall, which hissed when I pressed it. A communication device! If I talked into it, my father's fiancée—who happened to work in that hospital as an administrative assistant—would be able to hear me! I thought she disliked me and my brother because we had a tendency to speak Hebrew in front of her children, who couldn't understand what we were saying. She must have thought I was possessed by the devil! *That's* what was going on! That's why I was locked up! I leaned on the button, sobbing, "I'm not possessed! *Please* make them let me out!" It didn't work.

I stuck my finger up my bum and wrote mystical symbols on the wall with shit. If I somehow came up with exactly the right combination of symbols, the door would open, and I'd be free. That didn't work either.

After a long time, I hit upon the magic words that would actually open the door: I told them I understood that I was sick, and I was willing to take their pills.

They let me out into the ward. I was still completely crackers.

They gave me a pair of johnny gowns to wear—hospital gowns that tie up at the back. I wore one that way and another one on top of it, tied at the front. I'd run after my doctor (at least, they told me this was my doctor. I only ever saw him in passing, when he was on his rounds) and say, "Please! I need my clothes! I need my shoes!" And he'd say things like, "Look at you! You're shaking. You're crying. You're obviously not ready."

They had me on a drug called Haldol, which I later found out was a neuroleptic. It made my muscles spasm. It hurt to move, but I couldn't keep still. My hands and feet twitched. My face convulsed. I drooled when I lay down. My skin was so dry it was coming off in flakes. I was horribly constipated.

The Haldol didn't touch my craziness, though.

When I was finally allowed to wear a housecoat and slippers, I celebrated by running away. I waited for a moment when the door happened to be unlocked and nobody was looking. I shuffled down the street a couple of blocks to my father's place and buzzed his apartment. He wouldn't let me come up. Eventually he came downstairs and I was let into the superintendent's apartment. Then the police came and took me back to the hospital. No one had even told me that I'd been committed.

The academic year had just begun. I found out that the faculty had gone on strike. There were no classes. I knew this meant they were waiting for me to come back to school. I made my father promise he'd get me out by October such-and-such, which was when I thought the strike would be over. The date came, and he didn't get me out.

One of my father's rules was that you never, ever break promises. That's part of why I'd always loved and respected him. But now he had broken the most important promise he'd ever made to me. By the time I forgave him, he was long dead.

His visits were terrible. He'd hold my hand and gaze into my eyes, obviously scared and miserable. I'd sit silently and wait for him to leave. When my mother came (as she did almost every day), it was completely different. She'd put on music and dance with me. She made a huge effort to act cheerfully and normally. I loved her for this. But she was always asking me to walk properly; I dragged my feet and walked with my arms held stiffly, upper arms against my sides, elbows bent and hands out in front of me. This was known among some of the patients as "doing the Haldol Shuffle": it was caused by the drugs. I hated being asked to walk like a normal person, because I couldn't do it.

The ward was a square built around a courtyard that was decorated with big, bowl-shaped concrete planters, each with flowers of a different colour. Sometimes I ate petals. Sometimes I dried them, rolled them up in cigarette papers and smoked them. They made me high. It was magic.

I made friends among the patients. There was a porch swing in the courtyard. I liked to sit there with my women friends, swinging and talking. Sometimes we'd laugh. Sometimes we'd even sing.

This was the kind of thing that kept me going.

Months went by. Eventually, despite the drugs and the terrible environment, I stopped being crazy. Boredom and the passage of enough time can do that. All the magic shrivelled up and withered away. I was no longer in an amazing new universe; now I was just another zombie on Haldol.

I got a pass for Christmas and went to my boyfriend's house. Not John— Jay, whom I'd been going with before I'd fallen for John, and who had stuck by me and been one of my few visitors. I was so scared of being out of the hospital, being around people who lived in the real world, that I hid in his bedroom the whole time.

Eventually Dr. Kaplan decided I was well enough to be released. I was still on a massive dose of Haldol. They sent me off with a big bag of pills. I went to live at my mother's place.

I was crazy when I got locked up, but not sick. Now I was definitely sick. I hurt all over. All I could do was sleep, eat and watch TV. I'd watch any old thing—game shows, soap operas—stuff I'd never have dreamed of wasting time on in my old life.

I slept over at Jay's sometimes. Once I got up in the middle of the night and walked, naked, across the townhouse complex where he lived, and sat in a sandbox and wept. It didn't matter what I did, because everyone knew I was nuts. No one came by, anyway. I brushed the sand off myself and went back to bed.

I kept seeing Kaplan every two weeks. I'd go into his office and he'd say, "How are you today, lass?" I'd say, "Fine." He'd ask if there was anything I wanted to talk about and I'd say no. We'd sit silent for half an hour, and then I'd go home.

Wandering aimlessly down the street one day, I realized that I felt as if I'd died and gone to hell. The bright, creative, joyous, promising young person I'd been the year before—the person I used to think of as "me"—had been crushed out of existence. In her place was a debilitated mental patient, gazing through windows at women who were slinging burgers or operating cash registers for minimum wage, wishing desperately that she could pull herself together enough to do that one day.

A couple of months later, Kaplan arbitrarily decided to switch me from Haldol to chlorpromazine (another neuroleptic). He put me back in hospital for the switch. I was scared—what if they decided to keep me there? Each time I was given a chlorpromazine pill, I put it under my tongue and then spit it out when no one was looking. Most people who go off these drugs cold turkey experience horrible withdrawal symptoms, including "psychosis," but I was lucky and didn't.

They let me go. Needless to say, none of the problems that had driven me crazy in the first place had been addressed by the professionals in charge of me. And yet, unaccountably, I started feeling better. Then I started feeling a *lot* better. I was getting all excited. I was going to start a business! Silk-screening these brilliant T-shirts I'd just designed. I borrowed a hundred dollars from one of my father's ex-girlfriends, with the intention of buying equipment and supplies. But the business never happened, nor did I ever pay her back.

I'd stopped seeing Dr. Kaplan, whom I hated. Now I was seeing Dr. Sadavoy at Mount Sinai Hospital, downtown. He seemed nice enough, but we didn't communicate at all. As with Kaplan, he'd ask me how I was and I'd say I was all right. Then we'd stare at each other till the end of the appointment. I entertained myself by trying to see if I could keep from blinking longer than he could.

One day I was visiting my friend Karen and she said she had something to tell me. "I'm gay," she announced. Much to my own surprise, I blurted, "You're just saying that to get me excited." She was offended and wanted me to leave, but I persuaded her to go to bed with me instead.

Bliss! *That's* what had been going on all this time! It wasn't that I couldn't find the right man; it was just that men didn't do it for me. I was gay. Wow!

How fabulous! I had a clearly defined identity. (This fell through soon afterwards, when I reverted to bisexuality.) I told anyone who would listen that I was a homo and launched into an intense relationship with Karen. Too intense for her. She stopped calling me.

Not long after that, I was back in the universe of good and evil forces. I called Karen and, about a hundred times, told her that I loved her. But one day soon after that I called, and a roommate informed me that she'd left town.

I was obsessed with her, and at the same time started being obsessed with John again. I lay in bed with the radio on my belly and he talked to me through it.

I was staying at my mother's place at the time (she was in Israel). I was living on one lima bean a day. I knew this was all the nutrition I needed. I got very skinny, which pleased me. I stopped sleeping. One day I put a lima bean in an empty wine bottle and threw it off my mother's eighth-floor balcony. I knew that this would save the world. It didn't, although it did dent the top of a car. Fortunately, the car was unoccupied.

For some reason, my high school friends Beth Raymer and Stephen Stuckey seemed worried about me. They sometimes slept over. I kept asking them what was going on and they kept saying nothing was. I observed that Stephen often turned into Beth during the night, which was interesting.

At some point Stephen told me I should read the writing on the wall, and I started doing just that. It was a good thing I did, since it was all personal messages for me from powerful, mysterious forces. I was also in psychic communication with newscasters on TV. If I stared at them long enough, I could make them crack up laughing.

Looking out the window, I saw a UFO. It was brilliant, green and still. It made me happy. A single leaf on a plant in my mother's apartment turned dazzling gold, and I knew it was magic. At night I played a wonderful game with beings from other dimensions. We held hands and jumped off stars into space.

One day I phoned a graduate student of my father's and asked him to come see the movie *Alien* with me. At the cinema, I kept getting up and going to the bathroom and fiddling with my contact lenses. I threw one of them away. I couldn't concentrate on *Alien* at all. I left and went on a long, long walk through the suburb where the theatre was, which was not the one I lived in.

I ended up in the lobby of an apartment building, very late at night. No one was around. I needed to get rid of things. I dumped everything in my bag—a book, some paper, pens, aspirin, contact-lens container and cleansing solution, my umbrella, my key—onto the floor. I peed on the floor. I got rid of all my clothes except my shorts and T-shirt. I took out my one remaining contact lens and dropped that on the floor as well. Then I commenced the long hike home. On the way, there was thunder and lightning, which I knew was really Stephen Stuckey telling me he loved me.

It was morning by the time I got to my mother's building. I couldn't get in because I'd dumped my keys. I sat in the lobby waiting to see what would happen. A policeman arrived and asked if I knew a Mister Stickey. I said yes. He said Mister Stickey wanted these things returned to me, and handed me my bag, which had all my things in it, including my keys. I thanked him and went in, delighted with this evidence that the powers that be were helping me do what I needed to do. I didn't tell anyone about this.

One day Stephen and Beth told me we were going for a cab ride. I said, "Oh no we're not." I knew something was up, and that it wasn't something good. But they weren't taking no for an answer. They bundled me into a taxi. I whipped my shoes off and hurled them out the car door—if I didn't have my shoes, they couldn't make me go. But they retrieved them and stuffed them back into the cab with me, and we ended up at the Mount Sinai emergency ward.

Next thing I knew I was in a wheelchair, wheeling myself backwards really fast, thinking I could get away. I backed myself into a corner. Déjà vu! I was grabbed, stripped, shot up and tied down. Very quickly, I was back in solitary confinement. I yelled a lot and, after I was unbound, spent a lot of time banging on the door. History repeated itself. I agreed to take their drugs and they let me out onto the ward.

There was one nice nurse, Nina. She is the only psychiatric nurse who ever treated me like a human being. One day she suggested it might make me feel good to have a shower. I guess I'd been there for a while and smelled pretty bad. I was too scared and said no. But she gently and patiently persuaded me. I was so drugged I couldn't move very well, so she helped me into the shower and washed me. Being touched with kindness made me cry.

Some of my fellow patients were beings from different realms. Two in particular, a young man and woman, were both quite beautiful in an elfin sort of way. Neither of them ever sat down in an armchair or couch; rather, they'd always perch on the arm. They were magic.

One day I was taken off the ward to go to the Occupational Therapy room for the first time. The ward was very drab, but the OT room was full of colours. It freaked me right out. I huddled in a corner whimpering until someone escorted me back to my room.

I saw my doctor occasionally. Not Dr. Sadavoy—this one was a woman. She was very beautiful, but distant and cold. Because the drug that I was on, Nozinan (which is a lot like Haldol), caused severe constipation, I frequently had to be "disimpacted." My doctor would put on a rubber glove and scoop my shit out with her finger. Shades of unsuccessful magic rituals! But this worked, and had nothing to do with magic.

This doctor told me I had a disease called schizophrenia. Apparently I'd always had it, and there was no cure. I'd have to be on Nozinan, or something like it, for the rest of my life: otherwise, any time I was under stress, I'd have another psychotic episode and have to be hospitalized again.

I never talked to her about my life or how I felt. It didn't seem safe.

Again, I stayed crazy for months. Many times each day, sitting in the day room, I'd suddenly announce, "I have to go obsessive-compulse my teeth." This was supposed to be funny, but no one ever laughed. I'd head for the bathroom, and often actually brush my teeth. Sometimes, though, I got lost: I'd forget where I was and why, and stand staring into the mirror for a long time.

I found a bag of sweet popcorn, all different colours, in my roommate's dresser drawer. Each different colour was a different drug. Pink ones were acid, yellow ones pot, green ones speed. I ate popcorn and got blasted.

Every day I'd go around and around the ward, very fast, to work off the restlessness from the drug. Once a nurse grabbed my arm and snarled, "You're speeding." I shook her off and went around again. Again she said, "You're speeding." I said, "So give me a ticket," and just kept moving. The next time I came by she said, "If you don't stop that, we're going to have to give you electroshock."

I stopped.

My roommate, a sixty-one-year-old woman, had been put away by her children as a "manic-depressive" because she'd been spending money they felt she should leave to them when she died. There was nothing wrong with her when she was admitted. Her children were able to have her committed because spending lots of money is actually a documented "symptom" of this supposed disease. She was my friend. Every morning, I'd wake up all of a sudden and sit bolt upright, gasping, sure I was having a heart attack. She'd come over to my bed, hold my hand and tell me I'd be okay. One day I wrote her a note saying, "Thank you for saving my life every morning." She was embarrassed. She didn't think she'd done anything.

She wore bright pink leotards and a matching T-shirt with the signs of the zodiac on it, and the staff would say to her, "Look, you're sixty-one, not sixteen. You're dressing inappropriately." After a while, they started giving her electroshock. Lots of it. Several mornings a week she left our room early, and they'd wheel her back in on a stretcher some time later, unconscious. When she came to, she'd have no idea where she was. After a while this kind, spunky woman became a silent, burned-out shell.

So I knew about shock. The day after the "speeding" incident, I said to my doctor, "I understand you're planning to give me shock treatments." She said, "Oh, no. We'd never even think about doing that without discussing it with you first." Years later, I found out my doctor had been harassing my mother for some time to let her give me shock, because I wasn't "responding" to the medication. But my mother wouldn't allow it, and I'll always be grateful to her for that.

For a long time I was not allowed visitors. The official reason for this was that it would upset me too much. However, I think it was because they didn't want anyone who might care about me to see how messed up I was on their drugs.

"Life" in the bin

As long as I was crazy, I wasn't bored, because there were things happening all the time. But eventually, again, enough time passed that I stopped being crazy. I realized that in fact there was nothing happening, and it all became unbearably tedious.

I got very used to living in the hospital. The first time I was taken on a group walk, I was so deeply shocked by being out on the street that I had to go back right away.

After I became accustomed to going outside, they sent me to Vocational Rehabilitation at Sunnybrook Hospital, a long bus ride away. My first day there, they gave me a typing test—I used to type sixty words per minute. They subtracted my mistakes from my score and told me humourlessly that my typing speed was now minus six words per minute.

They tried me on a cash register but I couldn't get the hang of it, so I ended up standing up all day, turning the crank on an obsolete Gestetner copying machine. I hated Voc Rehab. Fortunately, they only made me go there for a few weeks.

I wanted very badly to get high and couldn't. Friends came and took me out for walks and smoked me up. I snuck off the ward with other patients and went drinking. But I was unable to alter my consciousness; somehow, nothing got me off—not that I ever stopped trying.

I made a lot of friends on the ward. Judy was a dyke and a real sweetie. She was completely sane, but sad sometimes, because she'd had a lousy life. Her diagnosis, of course, was clinical depression. But she was often lots of fun. Lorraine was a very young woman from Manitoba, full of humour and always trying to make other people feel better. Penny, a talented cellist, once let me do a nude drawing of her. Every evening Penny was given a sleeping pill called Dalmaine, which she really liked. Sometimes she'd put it under her tongue and, when the nurse went away, take it out of her mouth and give it to me.

Every day I talked with Penny and with other women patients who were convinced that they were bad people. All of them were perfectly nice people, but had been persuaded otherwise. I think it was often some combination of growing up female, being screwed around by their families and by men, and what happened once they were in the hands of the "helping" professionals that made them so mixed up.

Many of my fellow patients were sad or angry, but not particularly strange. But some of our keepers were obviously cracked. One of the orderlies regularly threatened pretty young female patients with rape. Another, alone with the patients at night, would say, "Now I do disco for you." He'd put on cheesy music, stand up on a table and do a wiggly little dance. He always wanted to play this free-association word game with me when I was up late and everyone else had gone to bed. He'd say a word, and I was supposed to respond with the first thing that came into my head. I hated it. He called it therapy, but I felt he was trying to manipulate me into saying something dirty.

Long before sunrise, the nurses would come on their rounds, shining flashlights in our faces, waking us up. They'd yell at us if we wanted to lie down during the day, even though there was nothing to do and the drugs made us exhausted all the time. I kept asking them to reduce my medications, because they made me feel so terrible. Eventually they did. I was on Stelazine (another neuroleptic) by then, and fifteen milligrams felt like nothing to me, after being on sixty.

In April, they decided I was well enough to leave and that I should look for an apartment. I found a nice, cheap one and came back and told them. Alas—my "treatment team" (my doctor, the head doctor, my primary nurse and my social worker) had had a meeting meanwhile and come to the conclusion that I wasn't well enough to live on my own after all. Instead, they'd decided to release me into a group home for psychiatric patients. They sent me to a new shrink, outside the hospital, and he gave me a hundred tablets of Stelazine and a hundred of Imipramine (which is an antidepressant—someone had noticed I was unhappy).

Regeneration House was full of people who were in far worse condition than I was, because they were on much heavier doses of drugs. No one seemed crazy, but most were so drugged they could barely move.

At age twenty-two I seemed destined to spend the rest of my life going back and forth between the group home and the hospital, like other long-term patients I knew. Obviously, there was no point in going on. The only sensible thing to do was die.

As it turned out, killing myself was the first thing I'd been excited about for ages, and I couldn't wait long enough. I ate my two hundred pills at seven in the evening, with a few glasses of water (and a litre of chocolate ice cream, to celebrate). At last, after all those months, I got high—a dreamy, drifting, beautiful high, all the sweeter because I knew I'd never have to come down. When my roommate came upstairs at ten, I was unconscious and convulsing. I was taken to the nearest hospital to have my stomach pumped. Then it was back to Mount Sinai, where they told me I'd have to stay for quite a while longer, since I was obviously still sick.

Obviously.

Now I was mad, and I don't mean crazy. I started engaging in Inappropriate Behaviour. My doctor found me smoking pot on the ward, called me into her office and screamed, "How dare you medicate yourself?" My treatment team decided to send me to a loony bin in Southern California, near the ocean, which sounded great to me. The official reason was that there weren't enough Activities to keep me busy, either at Mount Cyanide (as I'd now dubbed it) or, in fact, at any hospital in Canada. We only had Activities (OT and Ceramics) twice a week, and they said I needed a full schedule in order to be sufficiently stimulated. But I strongly suspect they wanted me out of there because I was just too much trouble.

One day I set fire to a historical romance someone had given me. I put it in a metal garbage can first, in the middle of the room. Aside from the fact that I couldn't stand romances, one of my roommates was in the middle of banging her head on the wall till it bled, a favourite pastime of hers. She was getting all the attention, and I wanted some too. In Dr. Bukhari's mind, my action constituted a threat to the entire hospital. An emergency meeting was called, and I was made to apologize to everyone on the ward for endangering their lives. So now, besides being a chronic schizophrenic, I was a firebug. They didn't take firebugs at the California bin, so my keepers decided to send me to one in Maryland instead.

A California beach was one thing, but a suburb of Baltimore was quite another, so I said no. The next thing I knew, they had me on Valium. Now, all the time I'd been locked up, I'd kept thinking, "Why don't they ever put me on something that makes me feel good? How come they just give me shit that makes me feel horrible?" Valium was fantastic: I felt relaxed and happy for the first time in what seemed like years. I agreed to the transfer. I would have agreed to anything. Of course, a few days after I arrived at Shepherd and Enoch Pratt Hospital (SEPH) in Towson, Maryland, they stopped the Valium. Luckily I hadn't been on it long enough to experience any withdrawal effects, other than severe disappointment.

SEPH looked like a country club. It was a low-security facility with wooded grounds, tennis courts, a swimming pool and a well-stocked library. It was very, very expensive. Long-term American patients stayed there until their health insurance ran out and then were shipped to nasty state hospitals. My Ontario health insurance covered only a fraction of the fee. There was only one reason I could afford to be there at all: my father had died the previous October.

My social worker at the Mount had come to my room one day and told me he was dead. It never for one second occurred to me to believe her. I was positive this was a test to see if I had the right reaction to that sort of news, and that if I passed I would be discharged sooner. Months later, I began to clue in that he actually was dead, but told myself I didn't care.

He had left me money, but as I had been declared mentally incompetent, I was not allowed access to it. Some of it had been stolen and squandered by an unscrupulous relative; some of the rest was being used to keep me in Maryland. Once I'd "earned" the "privilege" of being able to go off the grounds, I was given an allowance from a portion of that money.

Shortly after I was taken off the Valium, I realized that I would never see my father again. I went into the "side room" (the solitary confinement cell, which patients on my ward were allowed to use, unlocked, if we wanted to be alone) and howled, grieving for him. Some time later, I told my doctor about this, and used the word "howled." He said, "Oh, that's interesting. I didn't realize you were still psychotic when you were admitted."

My doctor told me that my new diagnoses were "atypical depression" and "borderline personality disorder." When I requested definitions, he said I was depressed but still capable of laughing at jokes, and that I was on the borderline between psychosis and neurosis. He also informed me that I was attracted to him, which was equally idiotic.

There were Activities for patients at SEPH from eight in the morning till four in the afternoon, five days a week. Art therapy, music therapy, dance therapy, water therapy (playing basketball in the swimming pool), and so on. One day I got a letter from one of my old roomies at Mount Cyanide, telling me that Penny, the cellist, had finally succeeded in killing herself. Taking no chances, she'd overdosed and then crawled into a full bathtub with her electric radio and turned it on. I was glad for Penny. I knew how hopeless she had felt and how much she had wanted to die. A nurse asked if I'd gotten a nice letter from home, and I told her my friend had killed herself. I was excused from Activities that day. I stayed in bed and read.

Penny wasn't the only one of my fellow patients to commit suicide. David jumped in front of a subway. Karen hanged herself on the ward. Jim ate Drano. I never found out how Thérèse died, except that it was by her own hand. All of them were on prescribed medications. All had had enough of life as mental patients.

The great escape

My ward at SEPH was kept unlocked, except when someone misbehaved. The staff didn't intrude on our lives all that much. They kept an eye on us, but they didn't harass us as long as we were good. It wasn't like the Mount, where the nurses were always trying to get us to talk about how we were feeling.

I made friends quickly, especially with this cute hippie boy, Carl, from Georgia. He told me within five minutes of meeting me that he was bisexual, and I told him I was too. We became lovers, and our relationship reminded me of why life was worth living. I decided to run away.

It was easy. On "movie night"—Saturday evening—I headed out for the building where the movies were screened, bag stuffed with books, letters and my diary under my arm. A staff member I passed on my way out the door said, "You look like you're going away for the weekend." I smiled and assured him that I was just going to the movie. I walked out of the building and kept walking, off the hospital grounds and over to Towson State University. I called a cab, giving a false name, rode into town and watched a Bette Midler film. It was movie night after all.

I'd been hoarding my allowance money for weeks, so I had more than enough for bus fare back home. I hit the station around midnight and got on a Toronto-bound bus.

Free at last!

Cruising through the northeastern United States on that sunny October day, I devoured the landscape with hungry eyes. I was out in the world again. I was so proud of myself and so happy. I wasn't afraid. All that mattered was that the future was wide open.

My seatmate on the bus, after a friendly exchange of first names, asked, "What do you do?" I told him I was an escaped lunatic. He changed seats at the next stop.

For years the community mental health industry has been putting out literature that tries to alleviate prejudice against crazy people. But these educational efforts have been based on the notion that crazy people are sick and that it's okay to be sick. This approach doesn't work. For one thing, not all physical conditions are stigma-free: for example, people who have AIDS or cerebral palsy—not to mention those labelled developmentally handicapped—are stigmatized as least as much as mental patients are. In any case, "the public" does not think that crazy people are okay, any more than it ever has. And we crazies are in no way helped by the belief, used to justify dubious treatments, that craziness is an illness.

David Cohen, an associate professor of social work at the University of Montreal, has done a lot to help clarify what's wrong with looking at craziness as sickness. David has degrees in psychology and social work, is the associate editor of *The Journal of Mind and Behavior* and has acted as editor-in-chief of *Santé mentale au Québec* (Mental Health in Quebec). His research interests focus on the use, effects and regulation of psychiatric drugs; ethics and the mental health professions; medicalization and social control; and the development of alternatives to psychiatry.

David Cohen

My interest in psychiatry dates back to my first experience as a social worker, in 1975. I had to take an elderly woman who was hallucinating to hospital, somewhat against her will. She'd ask me to take her there, and then she'd say, "No, don't take me, I never want to go there." She kept changing her mind. She was seeing grease coming out of everything. She'd open the taps or open a can of dog food and see grease coming out. You could see marks on her face where she'd tried to scratch the grease off.

But as soon as she got to the hospital, she stopped all her crazy behaviour immediately. At first it had seemed like she was swept along in this process of "psychosis," but the moment she arrived at the hospital, she was as sane as you or me. That gave me a different take on what I had considered to be mental illness. She had been assuming a role, mostly unconsciously, I believe. And when her needs were met she no longer needed to assume that role. It wasn't acting, but there was a sense of drama there. The context created "symptoms." She needed to act crazy to get to where she wanted to be.

She lived all alone, three floors up, and she had trouble moving. She blossomed within five minutes of being evaluated at the hospital. She seemed to be in her element. I found out later that she died in the hospital, not long after being committed. I was told that she cleaned herself up, put on some make-up, lay down on the bed and died. It seems to me, in retrospect, that she got herself admitted because she knew she was at the end of her life, and she didn't want to die alone.

In 1977 I worked in a youth court where I came into contact with the juvenile justice system and saw how psychiatry was used to label and control delinquent kids, and excuse violent kids. It was then that I really began to pay attention to psychiatry as an oppressive force.

In 1978 I published an article titled "Psychiatric Social Work and the Notion of Nonresponsibility," a very libertarian critique of the social worker's role in locking someone up against his or her will. It asked, "How can a profession whose code of ethics includes the need to respect a person's right to self-determination participate in involuntary commitment?" I was expounding on the ideas of Thomas Szasz and of John Stuart Mill. It was published in *Intervention*, a Quebec social work journal.

I continued as a social worker until 1983, then took a year off, travelled a bit and began to seriously study theories about schizophrenia. An article I wrote in 1983, which was published in 1986, set me on the course I'm following today. I simply went to see what the psychiatric literature was saying about schizophrenia. I read hundreds of journal articles. I asked myself, "What are they really saying? What's this dopamine theory? What do these neuroleptics do?" So I read and read, identified the contradictions, and wrote a paper which was eventually published in *The Journal of Mind and Behavior*.

I concluded that psychiatric ideas about schizophrenia are extremely reductionist. So much so that even if there were something distinctly biological in schizophrenia, psychiatry wouldn't be able to find it. Psychiatry's conception of biology is obsolete. It says, essentially, that genes program brain development, and the brain programs behaviour. This, in spite of, for example. the incredible advances that have been made in understanding how one's experience can alter brain structure. Biology is actually trivialized in psychiatry. Of course, the universe of social relations and meanings is also immensely trivialized. Based on current thinking, psychiatry will never grasp why people go crazy.

Drugs

The use of drugs like neuroleptics constitutes obvious, top-down social control of disturbed and disturbing people, using chemical bonds. Of course, in the very short term, this might prove useful to patients—and especially to those around them. But it certainly is not useful to the many "chronic schizophrenics" who go in and out of hospitals despite years of drugging.

In the days when lunatics were chained to walls, asylum wardens saw them as beasts or madmen. But at least they were responding to them. Today, with neuroleptics like Haldol or Modecate injected once or twice a month, psychiatry is moving further and further away from crazy people, and deeper and deeper into the infinite recesses of their brains. Living, thinking, feeling, angry, despondent people are seen as if they were nothing more than disembodied brains. It's absurd.

Psychiatrists react less to their patients than to drug companies, families, the media and insurance companies. Drugs and the whole technological world view behind the drug "solution" are making it harder than ever for psychiatrists to understand the people they say they're trying to help.

Sometimes I wonder whether psychiatric drugs should ever be prescribed. Sometimes I wonder whether every kind of drug—including LSD, tobacco and neuroleptics—shouldn't be made available to adults. I'm inclined to believe that no drug, no matter how dangerous, should ever be banned. And I'm not just taking a libertarian view here. I'm taking a very practical view. People like drugs. People want drugs. People need drugs. People use drugs. All kinds of drugs. Psychiatric drugs are not necessarily more dangerous than other drugs; they can be more dangerous or less, depending on how you use them.

I think it was [dissident psychiatrist] Lee Coleman who said that psychiatrists have long demonstrated their inability to make wise decisions about treatment. Yet one always hears that mental patients can't handle treatment decisions. I believe that patients know more about the drugs than psychiatrists do. Of course they lack some of the information that's in the research and the textbooks. But I think that if patients—even those who are "psychotic"—could choose for themselves how they want to use neuroleptics, they'd be much less damaged than they would by psychiatrists prescribing them. I see this as a perfectly rational, practical approach, from which we might even learn a thing or two about the interface between persons and psychotropic drugs, besides getting better clinical results than we are now getting from psychiatric prescribing.

Now of course that means that it's the consumer who gets directly pressured to use the drugs. This may or may not be good. But it is happening today anyway. Direct-to-consumer advertising is growing by leaps and bounds, whether for allergy pills or antidepressants. Mostly, though, it's still the doctors who get the advertising blitz, not the consumers. The consumer doesn't know what strategy has been used on the doctor by the drug company to get him or her to prescribe the pill.

Is it better to have the consumer—the one who actually swallows the drug—pressured with advertisements about psychiatric drugs? To have ads on television saying, "The next time you're crazy, remember, Haldol will turn off the voices better than Clozaril"? There are dangers in this approach. But I think it's a step in the right direction to envisage taking the controls away from all drugs, including psychiatric drugs, while at the same time enforcing very strict product labelling rules. That of course implies that the person taking the drugs is the person buying them, which is rarely true in cases of people with so-called serious mental illness. But all this points to the need for a penetrating look at the politics and the economics—the political economy—of the drug prescription situation.

When I went to Berkeley to get my Ph.D. in social welfare, I began doing research on the long-term effects of neuroleptic drugs on psychiatric patients. I pursued my interests in the social dimensions of drug use and in the effects of drugs. For four years, all I did was study neuroleptics and other psychiatric drugs. All I can say is, we are far from understanding long-term drug effects, which, in the case of neuroleptics, may be particularly disastrous.

Since 1988, I've been studying the ways in which doctors prescribe various psychotropics and how the drugs' therapeutic and toxic effects are perceived, or, if you will, constructed. Of course this is leading me to broaden my frame of analysis beyond doctors and patients, to include various actors in the drug situation. I'm looking at the entire system of drug production, promotion, prescription and consumption, through to post-marketing surveillance. I'm trying to tie in tools and insights from various social sciences. I want to understand why one-tenth or more of the people on this planet are using mood-altering drugs, often by prescription and on the basis that they are sick, rather than because they simply want the drugs. I'm looking at the systems that encourage the use of approved drugs: drug companies, doctors, public policy, medicalization tendencies, social forces, distress. The social determinants of drug use.

Dangerousness

I'm working with researcher and activist Paul Morin on a study of documents produced by an administrative tribunal (the Quebec equivalent of a review board) for people appealing their committals to psychiatric hospitals. Paul and I and Jean-Pierre Menard, who is a lawyer specializing in health issues, are studying how the notion of "dangerousness" was defined and used by the members of this tribunal between 1975 and 1993. We've obtained the records of the sixteen hundred appeals that have been heard and decided in Quebec. We're doing a quantitative analysis of about three hundred of them, and a qualitative, in-depth content analysis of about a hundred and twenty.

We're finding that the process of the appeal is arbitrary. There's a law that governs all these bodies that says you can only put someone away if they are dangerous. But the law does not define dangerousness. So, how is this law put into practice? Well, a person could be in one hospital one day and considered dangerous because he's threatened his mother or because he's kicked an orderly, and be kept in hospital. In another hospital, on another day, another person may be exhibiting the same behaviours but may not be considered dangerous, and may be freed. There are dozens of contradictions.

There are many examples of the law not being applied, but in fact, there's nothing to apply in the law! The law says, "Don't hold someone except if they're dangerous." But it doesn't tell you what it is you're supposed to do. This, of course, is left up to psychiatrists.

As soon as psychiatric logic gets in on the act, all kinds of things can happen. The law is officially aimed at protecting people and the review board is aimed at giving those who have been committed a fair hearing and ensuring that their rights are respected. But once you've been committed, there's a strong presumption that you're crazy. And, given the vagueness of the law, being crazy means being dangerous, if only to your own health. So, from a psychiatric point of view—and two psychiatrists sit on the three-member review panel—not taking your medications, not cooperating with your treatment and not seeing things as your doctors do becomes equated with being dangerous and deserving to have your appeal rejected! This has become obvious in the course of our detailed analysis of the documents, in which we look at how the documents are organized, the language used, what's said and, especially, what's missing. Every year thousands of people are committed, yet the actual workings of the review board are obscure. We hope to get a closer look with this particular study in order to help patients' rights advocates and to make the system more transparent and more accountable. The project has been funded by the Conseil québecois de la recherche sociale (the Quebec Social Research Council).

Several years ago, I started doing training sessions about psychiatric drugs in AGIDD [Association des groupes d'intervention en défense des droits en santé mentale du Québec, or the Association of Mental Health Rights Advocacy Groups of Quebec], as a consciousness-raising exercise. In 1992, AGIDD obtained a grant from Health and Welfare Canada to produce a guide to psychiatric drugs, intended primarily for psychiatric patients. It's in the form of a book, accompanied by a video. My role has been to supervise the gathering of all the data, as well as to write and edit.

This book will be a complete drug guide. Virtually all the kinds of psychiatric drugs legally prescribed today are described in great detail. For each drug, we include side effects, indications, therapeutic effects, the history of its introduction, how it's prescribed and who prescribes it. We also outline critical perspectives on the problems for which the drugs are prescribed and suggest alternatives when these are available or feasible. The information is taken from about twenty psychiatric drug guides already on the market, supplemented by hundreds and hundreds of articles in the scientific literature on particular drugs.

We've used information from Peter Breggin's *Toxic Psychiatry* and from *Dr. Caligari's Guide to Psychiatric Drugs* by David Richman et al.—all the sources we thought were relevant. [Breggin and Richman are both dissident psychiatrists.] We also interviewed "users" [the word used in Quebec for people who are or have been mental patients], including AGIDD members. We held meetings for them to come and talk about their experiences with psychiatric drugs. Tapes of what they had to say were transcribed, and about a hundred comments will be prominently featured throughout the guide, unedited except to remove names. People said things like, "I took it and couldn't get off the bed," "I felt glued," "My mouth was frozen." There are also comments on the mental health system, doctors, other professionals, families, and madness as it is perceived by those who have experienced it. Some of the people are still taking the drugs; some comments about the drugs are positive, but most happen to be negative.

We're also including a chapter on drug withdrawal. For every kind of commonly prescribed psychiatric drug, we suggest how to withdraw—what to do and what not to do—how to reorganize your life, how to divide up doses in various portions, how to minimize risks, the difference between relapse and rebound (in "rebound psychosis," withdrawal effects can make you think you're going crazy again)—the whole works. This chapter should be immensely useful in light of how little is available on this extremely important topic. It's much easier to get a doctor to prescribe pills than it is to get one to help you stop taking them.

By any standard, the information in this book is objective; it's information that's in the literature available to professionals today. However, in the guide we're producing it's presented in a critical way, free from the pro-drug bias so obvious among those who research psychiatric drug effects, who typically both prescribe the drugs and regularly receive grants and other compensation from drug companies. One point the guide makes is that information about drugs is not the property of any particular group of people. Professionals don't own this information.

The guide is written in very accessible language; we've hired someone specifically for that purpose. The guide is not just for users; it's also aimed at nonmedical practitioners, who I'm sure would like a reference work that is in lay language but gives them solid, complete information.

The chapter on lithium is one of the most complicated. There's a lot of information about blood tests and about lithium's dozens of side effects. This chapter was read by three users, one of whom is on lithium now. She's the one who appreciated it most.

To get feedback, I met with the readers for a couple of hours. I was very pleased with the responses. But some readers thought it was too pro-medical because sometimes the word "patient" was used. They told us to use the word "user," or the word "person." So the word "patient" is coming out.

One woman in particular who made this criticism also said that when she got to the end of the chapter she realized that it was not pro-medical. She'd never seen so much information about lithium in her life. At first she thought this must be pro-medical, but when she got to the part about the efficacy and the long-term studies, she realized this was not like the things she was used to hearing. She thought it was the most complete, useful thing she'd ever read.

[The drug guide was published in November 1995 by les Editions de l'Homme in Montreal, under the title *Guide critique des médicaments de l'âme* (*A Critical Guide to Psychotropic Drugs*).]

The tardive dyskinesia study

[Tardive dyskinesia, or TD, is a neurological disease caused by neuroleptics. The word "tardive" means late-appearing: often the disease doesn't appear until after the drug is stopped. Even conservative estimates by psychiatrists indicate that TD is very common in people who are kept on these drugs for more than a few months. It is characterized by involuntary, abnormal movements, especially of the mouth and tongue, but many parts of the body can be affected. People on the street who are assumed, because of the way they look, to be mentally ill, are often actually suffering from TD.]

In the 1991–1992 academic year, I sent out a questionnaire survey regarding neuroleptic prescription practices to about two thousand Quebec physicians. One thousand of them were psychiatrists. It was part of my research at the University of Montreal, funded by federal and provincial bodies, both medical and social.

The questionnaire's purpose was to elicit information from practising physicians about how they would prescribe neuroleptics to schizophrenic patients of various ages with varying degrees of TD who were presenting different schizophrenic symptoms. The idea was to find out whether these doctors were aware of the risk factors for TD, how they dealt with these risk factors and how they prescribed the drugs to these patients. Most experts and sources say that the use of neuroleptics should be discontinued as soon as signs of TD appear.

My study had been approved by the president of the Professional Corporation of Physicians of the Province of Quebec, who had given me an enthusiastic letter of support, a copy of which was appended to every questionnaire. I also had a letter of approval from the Dean of Research of the Faculty of Medicine at the University of Montreal. Each of these bodies had carefully looked at the project, the questionnaire and my credentials. They not only endorsed the study; they even said, in writing, that it could help improve mental health services in Canada.

But the board of directors of the Quebec Association of Psychiatrists didn't like the fact that the study was being done, especially by someone who had criticized several aspects of psychiatric drugging. So they sent out a memo to Association members, which in essence said, "David Cohen is not a medical doctor. There's no doctor working with him. And we think he's biased. We urge you not to participate in the study."

Now, the accusation of bias is a terrible one to make against a researcher. It implies that you might do all kinds of nasty things with your data, that you're blinded by your biases—that your results can't be trusted. As a researcher whose work is based on transparency and scientific method, I can't imagine a worse accusation.

The University of Montreal was supportive and provided me with legal help to defend my reputation. But how could the damage to the study be undone? Data collection had to stop immediately; one couldn't possibly continue the follow-up of respondents. With this letter going out to half of my sample, the conditions of the research were dramatically altered.

However, in the two weeks between the mailing of my questionnaire and the mailing of the Association's memo, more than a third of the psychiatrists and general practitioners had already returned their completed questionnaires. In fact, in those two weeks I received responses from more than six hundred physicians. They certainly didn't seem to have a problem with the study, and many thanked me for doing it and came up with all kinds of interesting comments and suggestions. My response rate is not what I could otherwise have obtained, but it's higher than 30 percent, which is pretty decent for a survey of physicians on a topic related to their very identity as doctors: drug prescription.

This problem wasted a whole year of my time, and I'm just now finishing the data analysis. It shows consensus between practising physicians on how to prescribe, but little adherence to guidelines stemming from research, especially regarding prescriptions given to older patients.

In the long run, the memo had no negative impact on my career. I asked for and got accelerated tenure in that same year. I've probably got more grants on drug-related subjects than I can use. I'm more and more in demand for consultation on these issues. I'm director of a research centre, studying the social aspects of health and prevention.

However, that letter did cause a major psychological chill effect when it went out. I was a young, untenured professor accused by a powerful professional association of being biased. For about a year, it put me behind in a lot of my work. But it's made me stronger.

I'm now working on an analysis of legal approaches in Canada to understanding TD. Why are there so few TD civil suits? Considering the number of people who have TD and the fact that it results from a drug, and that most people who take the drug are not informed that they can get TD, you'd think people would be suing. But I know of no TD suits in Canada, whereas in the U.S. there have been at least thirty. Is it just purely that litigation is a more popular avenue of redress in the U.S., or are there more specific obstacles in place here? We're in the process of analyzing why this is happening. The ultimate goal is to try to provide compensation for victims. And the first step in that is bringing the issue to the public.

"Challenging the Therapeutic State"

[This is the title of each of two special issues of *The Journal of Mind and Behavior (JMB)*, edited by David Cohen and collectively titled "Critical Perspectives on Psychiatry and the Mental Health System." There have been three reprints as of October 1996.]

I consider "Challenging the Therapeutic State" my major contribution to the movement. *JMB* is a scholarly psychological journal that specializes in articles dealing with mind, consciousness and so on. In 1988, I approached the editor, Ray Russ, about doing a special issue that would bring together the leading critics of what Szasz called "the therapeutic state," because I thought it was time.

All I could see was more and more talk of pseudobiology and drugs and mental illness and the *Diagnostic and Statistical Manual*. And I thought, what's happened? Did the whole stream of critical thinking and practice from the 1960s and 1970s get completely eaten up? Is it gone? I didn't think it was gone. I was still reading things on the subject. So I attempted to put together the people I knew who had something critical to say.

The first volume came out in 1990 and was very well received. Within it, I tried to gather all the critical streams I could think of. There were some traditional people, some wild-eyed radicals, a couple of ex-patients. I tried to cover several issues: treatment, ideology, women, kids. As a result, people got in touch with me. I made many new contacts with psychiatric survivors and others.

About half of the pieces in the second special issue, which came out in 1994 and is smaller than the first issue, are written by psychiatric survivors. Together, these two volumes represent almost every strain of criticism of the psychiatric system. Existential, social control, Szaszian, psychological, sociological, legal, Italian, feminist—we've got it there. These volumes make it clear that there are still people who are thinking very seriously about these issues, including respected scholars. My editor wants a Part Three, on alternatives to psychiatry. I don't know if it's possible, but I'll be glad to think about it.

One of my favourite pieces in "Challenging the Therapeutic State" is "Subjective combinations in psychiatric diagnoses," by University of Illinois sociologist John Mirowsky. Mirowsky analyzes traditional psychiatric diagnoses, and concludes that people's troubles are something like stars in the sky. We see these stars and we organize them into constellations.

But the constellations don't really exist. There are only the stars in the sky, which you can see from your particular standpoint and organize according to your preferences. Constellations are just pictures you've projected, saying, "Stopping there, this is the end of one constellation. This is the beginning of another one." A star doesn't naturally "belong" in a constellation, or think of itself as part of a constellation.

Mirowsky makes the argument that there are a lot of emotional problems, but how we categorize them is purely arbitrary. (This is, of course, an argument against the ridiculousness of assigning diagnostic labels to clusters of disturbing behaviours, and then acting as if each label represents an entity, independent of your judgement.) He then shows how a lot of the problems fit into a circle, with one blending into another. He shows this in a diagram that identifies the basic types of "mental illness" and how they relate to each other. It's a really different way of looking at troubles, and I think it's almost a revolutionary perspective, though much of it comes from questionnaire data gathered in ordinary, large-scale community surveys. The point is that it's not high technology that will save us. It's the questions we ask.

Critical psychiatry—psychological healing beyond bio-reductionism, call it what you will—is not dead. The strain of thought continues, and it's varied. It's no longer centred around a few charismatic individuals or prolific writers. Many people are still thinking seriously about how to bring about a humane system of help, free of the coercion, mystification and intellectual and other monopolies that characterize the mental health system today. But much of that critique, however sharp, remains impotent. We must not delude ourselves: we have a long way to go. I hope that we will be travelling much faster in the future.

Out in the world

I wish I had known back in 1980, when I first got out of the clutches of psychiatry, that there was an antipsychiatry movement. I would have felt so much less alone. Much later, I found out that there actually had been some antipsychiatry activists in Toronto then. But at the time, I had no idea. It would have helped a lot to know that people were asking questions, and had been for decades, about what psychiatrists were doing to their patients and why.

When I reached Toronto after escaping from SEPH, I showed up unexpectedly at my mother's place. At first she was scared about my having run away, but she soon decided I'd done the right thing. I'm proud of her for having come to that conclusion.

After a couple of days my doctor called and said I had to go back to the hospital because I was still very sick. I agreed to return, but only on the condition that I could go back to my old ward. I was missing Carl that much, and, after all I'd been through, I did not feel comfortable living with my mother as if I were a child again. But the doctor said that would be impossible. So I told him to forget it.

The remaining money from my father's estate had been put in a trust fund. I now had access to an allowance of $150 per week, doled out by a lawyer. I got a cheap room in a house downtown, and spent a long time just drawing pictures and smoking dope.

For a while, I didn't have very much to do with people, though I was never completely without human contact. I was still friends with one of the women I'd been locked up with at Mount Sinai, and with two of my former boyfriends. And my mother never stopped loving me and was always there for me.

After a few months, my inheritance ran out and I had to get a job. I scored a six-month contract doing clerical work in the Micrographics Department at City Hall, thanks to my friend Stephen Stuckey, who was working there as well. He and several other people at Micrographics were writing for *The Body Politic* (*TBP*, a very smart gay news magazine, which is unfortunately now defunct). It was through one of them that I first met Chris Bearchell, who was news editor of *TBP* at the time. I started hanging around Chris's house more and more. In 1984, she and I became lovers, and I moved in with her.

I was immersed in a sea of queers, and life made much more sense. The people around me were talking about things that actually interested me. I didn't feel like a misfit anymore. Here was this whole world of people who were much more fun than "normal" people, and I was welcomed as part of it.

Until this time, I'd gone to a series of therapists. I knew psychiatry was no good, but I still thought my problems could be solved by experts. I would come out of therapy sessions feeling even more depressed than I usually did. It was through my contact with "the gay community" that I finally realized that my unhappiness came not from something being wrong with me, but from many things being wrong with the social system. My society had taught me to expect and want and believe things that did not necessarily make any sense.

The communal house I now lived in was a hotbed of political activity. People would drop in at any time of the day or night to talk around the kitchen table about politics, and sex, and sexual politics. It was hectic, exciting, inspiring.

The years I spent at "Harmony House," as it was ironically called—and, in particular, my connection with Chris Bearchell—constituted the most important part of both my political development and my recovery from psychiatric treatment.

Hi diddley dee, an activist's life for me

In 1986, a friend brought to my attention a classified ad for the position of editor of *Phoenix Rising: The Voice of the Psychiatrized*, a Toronto-based magazine. I'd never heard of *Phoenix Rising*. I went to a bookstore, got a copy and was blown away. I was really mad at psychiatry. I thought it was outrageous that I'd been locked up, stripped, shackled, forcibly drugged and put in seclusion, and that I'd been told that I had a mental illness and would have to stay on neuroleptic drugs for the rest of my life. Exposing that kind of injustice was exactly what *Phoenix* was about.

I wrote a letter to Don Weitz, one of the people who had started *Phoenix*, applying for the job. I wrote that I had been "treated" for "schizophrenia," and made it clear that I felt that what happened to me had been completely wrong. That was good enough for Don. I had a quick interview with the editorial collective, and—boom! I got the job.

I didn't really know what I was doing, but it didn't matter. I had lots of help, not only from Don but also from Chris, who had plenty of publishing experience from *The Body Politic*. She became the designer of *Phoenix* for its last three years.

When the mental health system got through with me, I was sure I could never be happy again. But now everything was different: my life was full of wonderful people; I was getting paid for doing exactly what I wanted to be doing; and I was doing it well and getting lots of praise for it.

Before *Phoenix*, when I spoke about having been locked up and how awful it was, people would be very sympathetic and say a mistake had been made in my case, as I obviously wasn't mentally ill. Even though I would explain that I had been as crazy as anyone had ever been, with all the classic signs of what is called schizophrenia, I don't think people believed me. They didn't understand. Yes, I had been mistreated as an individual, but what had happened to me was still happening to thousands of others.

Now, I was no longer protesting on my own. It was sobering to hear other people's psychiatry stories and to realize how lightly I had gotten off. So many people had been locked up and drugged for years, or had had hundreds of electroshocks. So many had died. But there was a sense in hearing new horror stories, as hurtful as they were, of having more ammunition to use against the system.

Being responsible for editing a whole magazine never stopped being scary. Before each issue was due I'd go into a terrible panic, thinking, "I can't possibly do this. It's too hard." I'd spend at least a month running around in circles and not getting anything done. But the actual editing, when I finally got around to it, was easy and enjoyable—it was simply a question of making sure everything was clear and consistent.

And publishing turned out to be something I liked a lot. Suddenly, I had an audience. I could write an editorial and know that strangers were going to read it and perhaps be affected by it. Above all, it was good to be able to give a voice to people who had always been silenced.

For years, anger was my sole motivating factor. While I was working for *Phoenix*, I wrote an article about revenge that was printed in *The Blotter*, a small leftist publication edited by *Phoenix*'s typesetter. I wanted to get back at the people who had locked me up and "treated" me, and that's why I was doing the work I was doing. On the *Phoenix* editorial collective, there was absolute consensus that psychiatry had to be abolished. When people said, "What about alternatives?" some of us would say, "Would you ask for an alternative to concentration camps? This is just something we have to get rid of."

One of the people on the collective who *was* into alternatives, though, was Bonnie Burstow. Bonnie has been a feminist and an antipsychiatry and antifascism activist for decades. She was a founding member and co-chair of the Ontario Coalition to Stop Electroshock (which helped D. Ewen Cameron's "patients" get compensation for the damage done by his brainwashing experiments), and moderated "Phoenix Forum," an antipsychiatry cable TV series. She also helped found, and chairs, Resistance Against Psychiatry, a Toronto political group. Besides having written many articles criticizing psychiatry, Bonnie co-edited (with Don Weitz) *Shrink Resistant: The Struggle Against Psychiatry in Canada* (1988), and is the author of *Radical Feminist Therapy* (1992). In 1994, she directed and produced the video *When Women End Up in Those Horrible Places*, a documentary on the treatment of women in Canadian psychiatric institutions.

O

Bonnie Burstow

I had a minor interference in my life by psychiatry, but it was significant enough to scare the daylights out of me. It was a very close call; I could have had a lot worse happen to me, and I was lucky. Twice I was taken to a psychiatric institution against my will, and both times I got out within six hours. I got out intact, but it was scary.

My father had been subjected to more than a hundred electroshocks. He thought it was a good thing, but I sure as hell didn't. He suffered from memory loss, which upset him. His reaction to being upset was to get violent at home. So, indirectly, psychiatry had a huge effect on my life.

One day a nurse from the Queen Street Mental Health Centre [Toronto's provincial mental hospital] got in touch with me and said, "They've just killed somebody else." She knew that I was critical of psychiatry and had some political connections. I arranged to get the files from her. We brought them to the New Democratic Party and had the matter raised in the House of Commons. And that's how I became involved with the antipsychiatry movement.

A few years later, I became a member of the *Phoenix Rising* collective. That felt really good, because *Phoenix* was a vital source of deconstructing psychiatry and got to so many psychiatric survivors who hadn't had a clue that anyone else had a critical view.

Then in 1983, I and a few other activists formed the Ontario Coalition to Stop Electroshock. Although it did not stop shock, the coalition set a climate of protest and the government had to listen.

Then Don Weitz and I started Resistance Against Psychiatry (RAP). Our aim has been to unite an understanding of different types of oppression with the anti-psychiatry perspective, while not budging an inch from the abolitionist position. We have also focussed on abolishing prisons. We've staged demonstrations against shock and held educational sessions on women and psychiatry. One of our most successful events was a showing of my antipsychiatry video, *When Women End Up In Those Horrible Places*. We packed a large auditorium.

I felt that it was important to bring out a video about what happens to women in the system, partly because there are some unique aspects to women's experiences. I wanted something that reflected the experiences of women from diverse backgrounds; not simply white, middle-class, able-bodied women. There's an elite in every movement, including the psychiatric survivors' movement, and I wanted to break through that elite so that different experiences could be represented. And I did find women from different backgrounds.

I've also written a book, *Radical Feminist Therapy*, in which I explore, among many other things, the fact that we need to know how to deal with crises if we are to keep people out of psychiatric institutions. The word "crisis" means turning point; it's not necessarily a bad thing. It's an opportunity for people to work through things, to get in touch with themselves.

It's important to help the person involved stabilize herself within her crisis. The aim is that she stops freaking out, but remains in the crisis and works through the issues. I focus on helping the person get grounded, so she can stay out of trouble.

The person needs reassurance that other people are there. And those other people need to really be there, so it's not phony reassurance. There's nothing as scary as going through crisis all alone. You need people who'll stick with you through it. You need to know that anyone who's trying to help you is reliable, and will not turn you in to the authorities.

Ideally, there should be more than one person helping someone in crisis. That way, the person can know, "This one will call Monday, that one on Tuesday," etc. And she can depend on this for as long as it's necessary. Suddenly, the crisis stops being a freakout. It starts feeling different. Aside from just being there, a support person can help the person in crisis do basic, grounding things—like breathing. If she holds her breath, she's going to have a panic attack. If she's helped to breathe slowly and deeply, she'll start to feel grounded. That kind of thing can take the edge off a crisis, so that it becomes something she can experience and work through.

It doesn't take a therapist to help someone this way. It's a real problem that most helping is done by strangers, and that people pay money for it. We need far more sense of community. There's only so much anyone can do in an hour, anyway. An hour a week with a stranger isn't going to get someone through a crisis.

It's strange—we go to school and learn trigonometry, but we don't learn to help people get through crises. There's something wrong with what we're being taught.

The movement

One of the difficulties, I think, is that there's a large part of the movement that wants to look respectable. And if that's what you want, you tend to have a lot of trouble knowing when you're being co-opted. And the hard-core, real stuff can fall by the wayside. Social movements have always needed to say what to a lot of people would be unspeakable. When we stop being able to say those things, we're no longer at the cutting edge of anything. We've been bought and sold.

The movement is no more a single entity than is the Canadian feminist movement. In Toronto, there are many groups that don't like each other very well. I won't say everyone in the movement has to work together, because I think it's very important for people who have different beliefs to work on different things. I would not want to work directly with somebody who wasn't for the abolition of psychiatry. But there is room for all of us in the movement, and we shouldn't drum each other out or expose each other or act like we're each other's worst enemies. We have to declare a moratorium on hatred of other people in the movement: to say that we won't participate in it, and we won't listen to it.

We need to raise public awareness generally, so that people who are having trouble with their kids don't turn them over to psychiatrists. And people who love their kids very much do that. We need to bring accountability back to communities.

The arrogant activist

Besides our fierce passion for crazy people's rights, Bonnie Burstow and I share immense anger and indignation about the way psychiatrists treat people. In my case, that anger has sometimes stood in the way of my being as effective as I'd like to be.

Until this year, when people defended psychiatry or said it had saved their lives, I was scornful. I thought they were stupid, deluded and wrong. I was extremely arrogant. I was positive that anyone who didn't agree with me was a fool. My conviction was so strong because I was so deeply affected by what had happened to me and what had happened to other people. In fighting psychiatry, I felt that I was in confrontation with pure evil. (I still have a tendency to interrupt people in the middle of what they're saying if they use a word like "psychotic," because I don't accept that term. This is not useful. I should learn to focus on the content, not the words they're using.)

To be on the *Phoenix Rising* collective, I had to join On Our Own, the self-help group that published *Phoenix*. I only ever went to one meeting, which I found boring and regimented. Many of the people there were in terrible shape from being on too much medication. It was like being back on the ward. I felt that everybody there had been brainwashed.

When I became editor of *Phoenix* , it wasn't reporting much about On Our Own because it had long since been transformed from the radical group Don and some of his friends had started to a much more conservative body. The group ran a store and a drop-in centre. It was good in that it gave people something to do and even a bit of money, and it wasn't run by mental health professionals. But it seemed like part of the system; something that wasn't political anymore and certainly wasn't interesting to me.

On Our Own ended up kicking *Phoenix Rising* out. They felt that we were too radical and weren't speaking for the majority. There were complaints coming from the mental health establishment too—that it was damaging to suggest that there was something intrinsically wrong with psychiatry.

I think it can be very frightening to let go of the belief that you're sick; to let go of the dependence on doctors. Relinquishing responsibility for your life can be comforting and reassuring. And the idea that there's nothing wrong with your brain and that you need to figure out how to make your life better, rather than depending on experts to look after you, can be terrifying.

I never had to make such a decision, because psychiatry had never made me feel better. There was no good side for me, partly because I'd had a good life before I got psychiatrized. But for many people who felt they had benefited from hospitalization and psychiatric treatment, the kind of attention they got from the professionals was the most positive they'd ever had. I met people who came from backgrounds of hideous neglect or abuse and people who just didn't have anything really good in their lives who found a refuge in psychiatry. People who'd always been told they were bad, and then suddenly were told they weren't bad at all—just sick. It's strange, thinking about all the psychiatrized people who are told they're sick but still believe they're bad. I'd been brought up being told I was great. I didn't believe that I was, but it made me feel worse, not better, to be told I was sick.

In any case, I felt that the kind of people who went to On Our Own wouldn't listen to reason, and I wanted to talk only to people who would listen. People like me, who were angry about having been locked up. Professionals who were radical, or were dissatisfied with what they saw their colleagues doing, or what they themselves were doing, in terms of psychiatric treatment. And lefties of various stripes. I wanted nothing to do with people who were still calling themselves mental patients. But now I believe that it's important to try to communicate with the people who are still within the psychiatric system. They are the ones who need the information most.

The core staff at the magazine were Don Weitz, Maggie Tallman and I. Maggie is fantastic—a supercompetent, kind, funny person. She took care of bookkeeping, administration and circulation and was in charge of what little advertising we had. Maggie was the steady force who kept *Phoenix* together. She was always there for everyone, including the people at On Our Own. I could go whine at her when I was finding things difficult, and she always helped me.

Don Weitz has been active in what he calls the psychiatric survivor liberation movement for more than twenty years. Besides being co-founder of both On Our Own and *Phoenix Rising*, Don helped start the Ontario Coalition to Stop Electroshock and Resistance Against Psychiatry. With Bonnie Burstow, he co-edited the book *Shrink Resistant: The Struggle Against Psychiatry in Canada*. Since 1994, he has hosted and produced "Shrinkrap." Broadcast on CKLN-FM (a college radio station in Toronto), "Shrinkrap" is the only antipsychiatry radio program in Canada. Don Weitz has been a lifeline for many people who, before they found out about him, felt completely alone.

Don Weitz

My awareness of the need to speak out against psychiatric abuse started in 1951, when I was locked up for over a year in McLean Hospital in Belmont, Massachusetts. I was committed as an involuntary "patient" by my family. The hospital changed my status to voluntary after the first three months, when they decided I wasn't going to run away, I guess. But I was systematically humiliated, treated like an infant—I was twenty-one years old—and labelled "schizophrenic."

I'd been having a rough time in school, like a lot of young people. I didn't know what I wanted to do with my life and got very upset about not knowing, which is not unusual. And I suppose I said what might be interpreted as some impulsive or insulting things to my parents. They didn't know what to do with me. They thought I was going off the deep end. My grades were falling. I wasn't the good, middle-class Jewish son that I had been. I was acting weird. I said I wanted to join the Marines during the Korean war. All this convinced my parents that I needed treatment.

So, after seeing a Freudian psychoanalyst, I found myself in a sanatorium for a few months, and then at McLean, where I was facing locked windows and locked doors. I was given two months of subcoma insulin shock treatment, which terrorized the hell out of me and succeeded in making me conform and stop saying things conventional people might think were outlandish.

The treatments caused amazing hunger pangs. That's one of the effects of insulin. And it shakes up the nervous system like you wouldn't believe. But I had it easier than some people, because I wasn't subjected to a coma, except once when the staff were trying to figure out the maximum dose I could take. Still, I felt it was torture, and I told them so. And of course they wrote down my complaints as further symptoms of "schizophrenia."

After I got out, I thought I could enter the so-called mental health field and try to prevent these things from happening to other people. So I got an M.A. and became a psychologist. Over the next fifteen years, I did some research in psychology. I administered, scored and interpreted a lot of psychological tests, including I.Q. and personality tests. I had some serious questions about the validity of the testing, particularly in the cases of people from different cultures.

The last time I ever worked as a psychologist or called myself one was between 1970 and 1972. I worked at the Queen Street Mental Health Centre and helped set up its outpatient clinic. But I saw too many of my brothers and sisters being brutalized. Overdrugged every day; put in cold wet packs—wrapped up like mummies, in sheets soaked in very cold water. In 1972, I wrote a letter of protest to the chair of Queen Street's Therapeutic Standards Committee. As a result, I was labelled a troublemaker. I got no staff support whatsoever. And that's what convinced me to get the hell out of Queen Street and psychology. I decided to join the newly established mental patients' liberation movement, which was active mainly in the United States.

Nineteen seventy-three was the year of the first conference on human rights and psychiatric abuses, which was held in Detroit, Michigan. In 1974 we called it the International Conference on Human Rights and Psychiatric Oppression, and then a few years later it became the International Conference for Human Rights and Against Psychiatric Oppression. Ex-mental patients, as we called ourselves at that time, started getting together, sharing our experiences and talking about fighting back. We were educating ourselves about electroshock, psychiatric drugs, lobotomy, involuntary committal—and about organizing and networking.

We'd always have a public day of protest during the conference. I remember the first one I was there for, in 1974. We'd heard about very young children being abused on the back wards of a Kansas state hospital. The information came from a radical social worker there. He was telling us about terrible things—children being heavily drugged and put in solitary. We organized a march and got some press coverage.

That was a key time for me; it just turned me around, to see how much support there was. I'd thought I was alone in my protests. But people had started speaking out, like Leonard Roy Frank, a San Francisco electroshock survivor who is extremely knowledgeable about shock and was getting progressively radicalized. Leonard helped start both the newspaper *Madness Network News* [whose motto was "All the Fits That's News to Print"]. That was the first in-your-face antipsychiatry ex-inmate-controlled magazine in North America. It ran from 1976 to 1986. Leonard was also one of the founders of the Network Against Psychiatric Assault (NAPA). In 1978 he edited a brilliant book called *The History of Shock Treatment*.

NAPA organized mainly around lobotomy, shock and drugs, and reached a lot of people out in California. So many ex-inmates had been suffering from these treatments and been mystified about them. Just like today, the doctors weren't telling anyone the facts, so we had to educate ourselves and offer whatever support we could to our brothers and sisters, to help them deal with the terrible and often permanent effects of psychiatric treatment.

Not everybody identified themselves, as I do, as being antipsychiatry. I'm against all of the system. But people in the movement were usually very much against certain parts of the system. They called themselves mental patients, and then in the mid-1970s that changed to "ex-patient," or, for some people "ex-psychiatric inmate." And now people are no longer satisfied with that, and some people are calling themselves "psychiatric consumer/survivors." My god! There's no real choice around treatment, so I think the word "consumer" is totally inappropriate and demeaning.

There was nothing happening in Toronto. But there was the Mental Patients Association in British Columbia. That's what inspired me. Judi Chamberlin [one of the founders of the U.S. mad movement] let me know that there was a group out there. In 1973, I took a trip out west, stayed in one of their houses, and met Lanny Beckman, who started the group. I saw democracy in action and wonderful support. For me it was amazing to see how open they were. Psychiatric survivors who had previously been cowed into silence on the wards were speaking out about what the drugs were doing. They were getting into heavy radical talk, organizing demonstrations and protests, making financial decisions, controlling their own money, making long-range plans. It was just astounding.

And I thought, "If people can do this after they've been through the torture of psychiatry and incarceration—if people can be as strong as that—why don't we have more of these groups?"

On Our Own

Back in Toronto, I hooked up with Harvey Jackson, who was involved in a therapy group where I was a co-therapist. He and I and Bob Carson, another ex-inmate, got together and decided to start something to provide support and friendship for people coming out of the Queen Street Mental Health Centre. We thought that was enough, and I still think you don't need any more reason than that to start a group.

In 1974, we started the Toronto Area Psychiatric Patients Association. But that only lasted for three months. There was too much quibbling; we didn't really gel as a group. The big organizing started in 1977. We found some rent-free space at All Saints' Church. It was just a safe place where people wouldn't be hassled or threatened with reincarceration. People were worried, especially if they'd escaped from Queen Street, that the cops would come after them and take them back there.

And that was the first Ontario self-help group. We called ourselves the Ontario Mental Patients Association, after MPA in Vancouver. No social workers, psychiatrists or doctors started it for us. We were really a grassroots group.

There was no funding at first. We just talked. The only rules were no booze, no physical violence and no verbal violence: people weren't allowed to insult each other. I think we policed ourselves a hell of a lot better than they do in City Council, for example.

Then Harvey decided we should make some money for ourselves. In 1978 we got involved with a local flea market. We'd never done anything like this before. But Harvey was very outspoken and had a business sense. I had a pickup truck, and we'd collect stuff—amazing things that people would throw out. We'd load the stuff into my truck and sell it at the flea market on weekends. We also got donations. In two years, we made $15,000.

Carla McKague kept track of the books, thank god. We couldn't pay her or anybody else. Most of the people were on disability benefits or welfare. One of the men in the group hadn't said anything for two or three months, and Harvey got him up to the flea market, and he started to talk. He was meeting people and came out of his shell. He's now a manager at an electronics firm.

Carla donated hundreds of hours of work. We would never have got our first grant otherwise, because the funder—the City of Toronto—had to see that we were financially responsible. And she was in law school at the time. It was she and Harvey Jackson who helped keep On Our Own afloat in the early years. Harvey helped give an awful lot of people self-confidence. And Carla was so great, keeping track of the money and teaching other people some of the skills that she had. If someone wanted to learn about bookkeeping, she'd sit down with them and teach them.

I think we were the first self-help group in Ontario that started making some money for ourselves instead of just depending on handouts. Later, we applied for funding and got it, and became more bureaucratized. The split started to happen in On Our Own. We started publishing *Phoenix Rising*, and those of us who were working on that started having ideological conflicts with other people in the group.

Phoenix Rising

Phoenix was born in 1980. Carla and I agreed that it would be totally controlled by psychiatric survivors, and that we weren't going to accept any funding from the mental health establishment. We never did, because they are the oppressor, and we knew that once we accepted money from them we'd lose our independence. They'd control us and try to influence our editing; they'd be able to cut our funding any time.

Carla and I had a one-bedroom apartment: that's where *Phoenix* had its first office. Everything was typed and laid out in this little place. Cathy McPherson and Mike and Joanne Yale came on board. Mike and Joanne, who were both blind, also had experience in the psychiatric system. That was the first collective.

Not all the articles were written by ex-inmates, but we controlled the content. We did ask other people whom we respected and felt comfortable with to write on topics that we weren't knowledgeable about. But the only shrinks we ever published were Peter Breggin and Lee Coleman, dissident psychiatrists who supported the magazine's objectives and our struggle for human rights.

The only funding we got in the first year was from PLURA—the Presbyterian, Lutheran, Unitarian, Roman Catholic and Anglican Council of Churches [PLURA was set up to give money to organizations that couldn't otherwise get funding]. They gave us a start-up grant of $5,400, which went for printing and office supplies. No one got any salaries until 1984.

I think our major objective was to empower survivors like ourselves, who couldn't get published anywhere else. We reached out to institutions, psychiatric wards, prisons. We had people sending us material from inside.

Our print run for the first issue, I think, was 250 copies. We ended up with 1,200 subscribers. But a fifth of those received the magazine for free: no prisoner or psychiatric inmate had to pay to subscribe.

By the end of *Phoenix*'s second year, people started hearing about it and writing in from all over the country and from some of the sister groups in the U.S. as well. University professors were using our magazine and listing us in their references.

Maggie Tallman, who handled the circulation and the books, did thousands of hours of work for free. Without her, we would have folded much earlier.

Our last issue, in 1990, was on gays and lesbians. I think that was one of the most creative ones, and I think it was the first time that any magazine in Canada had focussed so strongly on the psychiatric abuse of gays and lesbians.

Aside from each issue having its own theme, the magazine was organized in what I call priority chunks. We had a letters section called "Write On," a column about electroshock called "Shock Waves" and a section on drugs called "Phoenix Pharmacy." And "Maggie's Bag"—tidbits of information that Maggie put together. We had legal section called "Rights and Wrongs," which Carla was in charge of for a long time. Whenever we heard about ex-inmates fighting back, we tried to get them to write about it. Otherwise, we'd document it ourselves.

We had a book review section called "The Bookworm Turns." And a section called "Mad News," where we talked about what was going on in the movement. We got the idea for that name from *Madness Network News*, which inspired us.

There was another publication at that time as well: *The Cuckoo's Nest*, a newsletter started by ex-inmate Pat Capponi here in Toronto. In it, Pat kept a register of people who died at the Queen Street Mental Health Centre. *The Cuckoo's Nest* was distributed free of charge. It included information about psychiatric drugs and had an emphasis on boarding homes. Pat put the spotlight where it needed to be: on psychiatric abuses and discrimination against psychiatric survivors trying to find a decent place to live. She exposed the massive building and fire codes violations and the vermin in the boarding homes. It was a very important publication.

Still, I feel that *Phoenix Rising* was the most political ex-inmates' publication ever to come out in Canada. And I'd like to say this about it: if I were starting a magazine again, I would not want it to be published by an organization. A lot of people in On Our Own resented the strong tone of *Phoenix*. They said it was strident and too antipsychiatry. Well, that's too bad. We've all been there; we've all been oppressed. But some of our brothers and sisters in On Our Own felt that we were too much against the drugs! Can you imagine that? Some of these people were walking around like zombies and didn't want to admit that they were oppressed or overdrugged.

I remember people from On Our Own calling me up and saying, "Don, when are you going to stop being so mad?" I said, "Probably when I'm dead. I will always be mad at people who oppress you and me in the name of treatment. I don't have anything to apologize for, and this magazine has nothing to apologize for. Because nobody else is doing what we're doing."

Lanny Beckman founded the Mental Patients Association in Vancouver in 1970 and published many articles on "mental health" during the 1970s and 1980s, in such magazines as *Canadian Dimension, New Directions* and *This Magazine.*

○

Lanny Beckman

Most of my views on psychiatry were developed during my youth, when I was an extremist—which doesn't mean that I don't still subscribe to some of them. In the main, though, I've come to see my youthful desire to change the world as a manifestation of self-defeating personality disorder, and I'm now more comfortable living on an imperfect planet where, for example, 15 million children die of malnutrition every year. My advice to young radicals is extremely limited.

In the fall of 1970, I was at the Burnaby Mental Health Day Clinic, a day program that ran from 9 a.m. to 4 p.m., Monday through Friday. In the first three months I was there, three people committed suicide, all on weekends. We started off one Monday morning session, and the head shrink said, "I have some bad news. Bill James suicided over the weekend." There were twenty of us in the program, and we mostly knew each other by our first names. There were two Bills in the program, and I found my eyes darting around the room to see which Bill was there and which wasn't. Other people were doing the same thing. There was something in that moment that said, "This is our common fate. Any one of us could be Bill. And we don't know who we are. We don't know which Bill is the dead one and which is the live one. There's something really wrong here."

I suggested that the people in the program put together a phone list so we could call each other. The staff was initially resistant—they felt that mental patients who socialized without the supervision of trained professionals might hurt each other. The irony, of course, was that three mental patients had committed suicide while supposedly under the supervision of trained professionals. So it was pretty hard to imagine mental patients doing much worse for each other. The phone list happened within a week or so, and people started phoning each other.

Bob Hunter was a radical hippie columnist for the *Vancouver Sun* (at that time it was reasonable to have a radical left-wing journalist at the *Sun*). And he happened, just then, to be doing a series of really scathing articles about Riverview [Vancouver's provincial mental hospital]. I wrote him a letter saying that I was thinking of starting an organization of mental patients.

At the same time, I became interested in getting more information—facts and statistics about the mental health world. I had a friend who was a librarian. About six of the people in the day program went to the library one Sunday afternoon, and my friend pulled out a lot of sources of information. We spent a couple of hours going through it and organizing it.

Bob Hunter responded to my letter within a day or so, saying that he was interested in doing what he could to help start our organization. So he did a column on this idea, which fit naturally into his series of earlier columns. He included my name and number, and my phone didn't stop ringing for days. I was immediately approached by all sorts of people who had been mental patients, who wanted to give things and do things. There was one man who had been hospitalized in

Riverview twenty years earlier, and had really bad memories of it. He had a farm about sixty miles from Vancouver and offered to let MPA use it rent-free. Another man phoned and said he owned a house in the city and asked if we'd like to rent it. I said that sounded great.

We had our first meeting in December of 1970, in that house. There were about a hundred people. There were lots of testimonials—people talking about the agonies that they'd suffered from what is called "mental illness" and how these had often been compounded by the treatment they'd gotten. It seemed as if these were stories that people had inside them that they could hardly prevent themselves from talking about. These were the core issues of their lives, and they had not had a forum in which to talk about them. So here were all these crazy people together, with common stories and common interests.

MPA was not looking for "healthy mental patients." We really wanted the doors to be open to everyone, especially the people at the bottom. People who slept in cars and burned holes in chairs with their cigarettes because they were too out of it. Many of the people who came to MPA had no sense of having any say in a group situation. They were totally powerless people. Professionals started sending people to MPA because they didn't want to deal with people like that.

I would say the one thing MPA really succeeded in doing was being democratic. People who were really down and out would walk in when a meeting was going on. They'd stand at the back or go get coffee. They must have seen what was going on as a zoo. Two or three months later, they'd be sitting in the meeting, yelling at us about what they thought about some practical issue. That's what it was about.

There was also a very strong anarchist impulse, which was part of the times, too—a suspicion of leaders and of organizations. Someone said at the first meeting that we should elect a president. I remember saying, "Why don't we just see if we can get along without having people with those titles?" We never did have a president, at least in the time I was there. It was amazing that MPA worked so well, despite the lack of a formal power structure. There was no ultimate authority.

Because I had a lot of radical ideas, I had a big role in articulating MPA's politics. But it was quite clear that there wasn't a correct line. Lots of people disagreed with me and called me a crazy socialist hippie. Those who shared my ideas tried hard to make it clear that these were not "the" correct ideas. MPA was mostly about creating a community.

Being a "service organization" meant that we had to seek money from the government. Very soon after MPA started, there was money. We decided we'd have some people whom we would pay, and that they would be elected. We groped around for names for them. "Coordinator" was the most neutral term we could find. There were drop-in coordinators—the drop-in was open twenty-four hours a day—as well as coordinators of housing, research, crafts, the newsletter and the office. People were elected at a general meeting for six-month terms.

By the time I left, in 1975, there were five houses and an apartment block. That's where most of the money went—into housing. That was the most important service MPA provided. The houses were run by the people who lived there. If they wanted a coordinator, which most of them did, they had to accept the person prior to the general meeting, where the whole group would participate in an election.

We did a lot of public opposition to psychiatry. We were very public in our literature and in media interviews about opposing involuntary commitment. I remember once I was in a TV interview with the head of Riverview. A kind of debate; a five-minute news blip. I was saying it was wrong to call it a hospital; that there were so many ways in which it was more like a jail. And he was talking about people being too sick to ask for help.

I think there was a rule that no mental health professionals could be coordinators. And I don't think MPA ever put out any literature that praised psychiatry in those days. I remember putting together a cover for MPA's newsletter, *In a Nutshell*, that had two cartoons. In one, Superman was saying to Lois Lane, "I don't think I can do anything here, Lois. It sounds like something has gone wrong with his mind. He probably needs some real help." In the other, Mary Worth was saying much the same thing: "I don't know, dear. I think that's something only a professional can deal with." The caption was, "Where Superman and Mary Worth fear to tread."

But we were smart enough to know what we could get away with. MPA was so important to so many people that it would have been wrong to say things that could have resulted in a loss of funding. So we were careful about how we put things. We wouldn't call psychiatrists butchers or anything like that. We had a feel for where to draw the line; we were diplomatic. I think we saw psychiatry falling into a number of categories, ranging from atrocities associated with coercive treatment to just not treating people well.

I don't like the idea of professionals. A professional is by definition a stranger. So in a psychiatrist's office, what you're really doing is talking to a stranger. Psychotherapy, in theory, is about wisdom. You don't learn that in medical school or in psychiatry school.

Psychotherapy is a fancy term for talking therapy, which is a fancy term for talking. And, in almost all cases, it's better to talk to a friend who loves you than to some professional you're paying or the government is paying. I think that when people are in a lot of pain they need to be with someone who'll love them. And you don't get love in psychotherapy.

Philosophical roots of MPA

MPA was an outgrowth of the same impulse that resulted in the beginnings of women's liberation and gay liberation. It was part of the radical times. And there were people like R.D. Laing around, saying that crazy people actually had some wisdom, that others could learn something from them. These were really extreme ideas. Wonderful ideas, which have disappeared now. Now we're living in the post-Reagan ice age. We live in a society of positive thinking, in which the worst thing you can possibly have is mental illness—what could be more negative than mental illness?

With the end of the 1960s and for real economic reasons, the political mood shifted, and a period of incredible reaction came in, spearheaded in the U.S. by the Reagan administration. So progressive movements, instead of trying to advance, were simply trying to defend themselves. The apparent backlash against feminism is the best example: ideas that were at one time seen by many as being obviously justifiable now had to be justified.

Most radicals didn't even know about mental patients' issues. But these issues were somehow piggybacked on women's liberation and gay liberation and other movements. So, with the conservative swing that began in the mid- to late 1970s and was consolidated in the 1980s, mental patients' issues ended up not just on the back burner but off the stove entirely.

There were a lot of things I wanted MPA to accomplish. And it did accomplish a lot. It provided housing for many people. It provided community for many people. But on the political stage, I wanted to see a real cut into the stigma of mental illness. And I'm sure the stigma is even worse now than it was then.

Language

I think the word "survivor" in the term "psychiatric survivor" is misused. A survivor, literally, is someone who really faced death and escaped. And most psychiatric patients were not facing death. I'll support the use of the term "psychiatric survivor," but I think it should be recognized as a metaphor.

We called MPA the Mental Patients Association to fight the stigma. We didn't want to use euphemisms or be anonymous. Plus, "mental patient" was a legal category. When you're in the hospital you're legally a mental patient. I love the word "mental." If a Martian were to come here and hear about a mental institution, he'd think you were talking about a university, because universities deal with ideas, and the mind produces ideas.

I believe that there's no such thing as mental illness. But there's something wrong with some people. What's wrong with them is that they experience great amounts of pain and suffering. They may or may not be weird. If they're not weird, they're called "neurotic." If they're weird, they're called "psychotic." They're called crazy: that's what "psychotic" means.

I have a friend who was at the Queen Street Mental Health Centre in Toronto when she was sixteen. She recently got her records and gave them to me to read. There were 150 pages. They talked about her as if she were a machine. One note accused her of having an "immature personality." She was sixteen years old!

One way of looking at psychiatry is that it's the medicalization of prejudice. And medicine is the secular religion of the age. So most people, when they see someone who is crazy or is in extreme and irrational pain—who has panic attacks or is too depressed to get out of bed for a month—say that that person is sick. Most don't even question the concept that such people are obviously sick. They're mentally ill. There's something wrong with their minds, and that "something wrong" is illness.

One of the problems with the concept of mental illness is the way the word "sick" is used. It's about as contemptuous a word as there is. If someone has done you some horrible injustice, you'll say, "He's *sick*." Or if you talk about Clifford Olson, who murdered twelve children, "He's *sick*." Inherent in the concept of mental illness is incredible hatred. That's one political reason why I don't accept the concept. Even if it were proven to me that there was mental illness, I would still say, let's get rid of the terminology because it makes people hate those who are called mentally ill.

It has a lot to do with concepts of mind and brain and how they're related. These are the most complicated philosophical problems imaginable. The issue of "mental illness" is basically a philosophical question that has political implications. Illness is a concept of the body, and to apply it to the mind, as Thomas Szasz says, is to mistake a metaphor for a fact.

A very common symptom in people who have coronary heart disease is feeling pain in the left arm. It's called "referred pain." Nobody will say that that person's left arm is sick. People will say the heart is sick. So if there's evidence that someone is suffering from some kind of brain "illness," the mental manifestations of it—anxiety, depression, hearing voices, thinking there are plots against you—are like the referred pain. The thoughts are not sick. There may be something in the brain that's wrong. But to think that the mind is ill is to annihilate the person.

I don't know what language to use. Depression, for example, is probably the least stigmatic of all so-called mental illnesses. But when someone says, "I suffer from major depression," or "I've been depressed for thirty years," the prejudice is right there on people's faces.

In this society, people who "go crazy" can either be given over to psychiatric care or somehow live in a society that is uncaring and lacks love. What MPA tried to say is, those are not the two choices. The real choice is to have a place to go where you're loved when you're crazy. That means building community. That's what R.D. Laing was talking about. I don't believe you should ever do anything to crazy people against their will. But those two choices—they're not choices. The word "choice" is often used for "alternative." It's like saying kids have a choice of either having their parents stay together and hate each other, or having the father leave. Those aren't choices. Those are alternatives. And kids never have any say in them anyway.

The one alternative we don't have is a loving place to go. The question of craziness would disappear if we lived in a humane world. Even if someone was in a state of incredible pain, the issue would not be one of diagnosis, putting a name on it, or calling it crazy or not crazy. Instead, it would be saying, "What can we do to help you?"

O

Mixed fruits and nuts

I believe that Lanny is right when he says that people need "a loving place to go to." I think we need this not only in times of crisis, but also to give us a strong sense of ourselves and our relations with others and to enable us to accomplish things and feel good, and so have fewer crises. A loving place was what I found in "the gay community": a place where I fit in and where people cared for me without wanting to change me.

When I was first editing *Phoenix Rising*, the most important people in my life were queers, not crazy people. My antipsychiatry work was a passion, but it wasn't my life. My life was the queer world.

Soon after I got involved with Chris Bearchell, she introduced me to someone she described as "one of the most interesting people I know." This was Ryan Scott, a talented writer, artist and bicycle mechanic. It turned out that, like me, Ryan had done time in the loony bin. Before long, I helped her get a job at *Phoenix Rising*. It was so nice having someone in my life who was part of both the queer world and the crazy world.

CMHA

In 1989 I got a call from the national office of the Canadian Mental Health Association (CMHA), asking if I would agree to be interviewed for a job coordinating their national consumer network. "Consumer" is a term that I believe was cooked up by the mental health establishment. It's short for "consumer of mental health care services" and is a euphemism for mental patient. The Ontario government had put out a document called *Building Community Support for People*, which emphasized the importance of "consumer participation" in the planning, delivery and evaluation of mental health services, and touted the idea of partnership between the "key stakeholders" in the mental health field. The stakeholders included "consumers"—but only at the bottom of the list, after government officials, mental health professionals and family members. (I still can't hear the word "stakeholders" used in this context without picturing a psychiatrist about to drive a stake through a mental patient's heart. But the stake is a syringe.)

There were a lot of dubious ideas in the report, like "patient identification and tracking," and "coordination of services." This was about the people who ran consumers' lives all being in touch with each other so consumers couldn't get away from them. But there was also an admission that the system wasn't working as well as it should be, and the suggestion for repairing it was to let consumers participate in running it. To this end, the CMHA had set up its consumer network.

Hugh Tapping, long-time antipsychiatry activist, was its first coordinator. Hugh has brought many people into the movement, and has written brilliantly about psychiatry and especially about electroshock, which he had experienced. Among many other organizing efforts, he helped found the Ontario Coalition to Stop Electroshock. Hugh had written for *Phoenix Rising*, and had read things I'd written for it, but we'd never met. Now he was leaving the network job. He gave them my name, and they called me.

I thought, "Now, here's a funny story to tell my friends: the CMHA offers Irit a job"—but that was as far as it went. I was rabidly anti-CMHA. Community mental health was supposed to be the "nice" part of the mental health system, but I knew better, thanks to people I'd met through *Phoenix*. Community mental health meant that instead of going to the expense of keeping you within walls and feeding you and hiring people to look after you, the professionals would just install the walls inside your head. You'd go to the community clinic and get patronized by staff and get your needle in the bum—a long-acting injection that would keep you under control until your next visit. The CMHA is responsible for reams of propaganda "explaining" mental illness and telling people that it can be controlled with drugs.

They also run "clubhouses"—psychiatric day-care centres for adults. When I was interviewing people for this book, several of them had a lot to say about the CMHA. Only a few, none of them living in big cities, had positive comments:

> "We get lots of support from the CMHA. I feel that we're all one. They've always been there for us and helped us through hard times. They come chat with us, and make us feel like we're all part of the same thing. And we're there for them, too. It's not just one way."

For the most part, however, CMHA "clubhouses" were seen as being vastly inferior to independent groups:

> "Our group gives us a place we can call our own. We're all equal. When you go to the CMHA, they make you feel like you're beneath them."

> "They have moods and it's normal, but if we have moods, it's a symptom of relapse. Everyone panics."

> "CMHA staff are on a power trip. They control the place, and make you feel like you're being baby-sat."

> "I feel depressed when I'm in the Clubhouse. In our survivors' group, you walk in, people are laughing and having fun. At the Clubhouse, it's all doom and

gloom and you ask yourself, 'Why did I come here?' Everyone is withdrawn. Trying to have a conversation is like talking to a wall. A lot of people go there for the lunch because they have nowhere else to go. Someone picks them up from their Home for Special Care, then takes them back there at the end of the day."

One person who worked for the CMHA as a token "consumer" didn't like what she saw at the organization:

"I think that they waste tons of money on useless projects. They get most of their sustaining grants on the assumption that they're doing something for us. And I think that they waste that money on shit that has nothing to do with us.

"A lot of their projects are misdirected, like this big depression campaign. 'The ten signs of depression—if you have these, you're depressed.' They have a 1-800 number you can call for information. It's really medically based.

"They talk about 'consumer participation,' but there were five positions available here last spring. Two project managers and three support staff. And I said, 'Gee, why weren't those positions filled by consumers?' And I was told those positions 'didn't need consumers.' Which means they were positions to do with mental health. And we can only work on stuff that has to do with mental illness. So, I said, 'What about the support staff?' 'Oh, well, those were summer jobs.' Like, consumers don't go to school, right? We don't need summer jobs."

I certainly wasn't considering taking the CMHA job. But then I talked to a good friend of mine who said, "Don't be a fool. Tell them you'll do it for $40,000 a year. Then you can be a spy." So I called them back and got interviewed. In the interview, I spoke quite frankly about my political views regarding psychiatry. I didn't see any reason not to, since these would soon become evident if I was hired. I also told them I was a dyke. I don't know exactly what it was that they didn't like, but they didn't hire me. Thank god.

Women and Mental Health Conference

When I was invited, as editor of *Phoenix Rising*, to speak at a conference called Women and Mental Health, in Banff, Alberta, I didn't yet know whether I'd be offered the CMHA job. It was May 1989, and the conference was sponsored by—guess who?—the CMHA. I took Ryan along with me. I was nervous about going by myself. The people who attended this conference were feminist mental health professionals, social workers, transition house workers, and so on. The only male speaker was Jeffrey Masson. He spoke to an audience of feminist therapists about how the whole idea of therapy was a problem because of the inherent power imbalance. I thought he was going to get lynched. I also thought he was one of the best speakers at the conference.

Another highlight was a performance by Mia Blackwell, a very talented writer and actor from Toronto who had been locked up. Her show was the coolest thing. She had a plain screen for a backdrop and a bed and chair for props. She'd keep going behind the screen and then coming out as a different character. She played a nurse and several different patients. The use of lighting and music was brilliant, as were the script and Mia's performance. Her show confounded the mental health workers at the conference, I think. It certainly boggled my mind.

I led a workshop at this conference together with Carla McKague, the woman who had started *Phoenix Rising* with Don Weitz. Carla had had electroshock and later became a well-known lawyer for people with disabilities, working mainly in the area of mental health. With Harvey Savage, Carla co-authored *Mental Health Law in Canada* (1987). She spent seven years as head of litigation for the Advocacy Resource Centre for the Handicapped, specializing in mental health test-case litigation. Carla has served on numerous committees, including the Committee to Evaluate the Psychiatric Patient Advocate Office, the ECT Review Committee, the advisory committee to the Commission on Advocacy for Vulnerable Adults and the Inquiry on Mental Competency. She currently works for the Office of the Public Guardian and Trustee (Government of Ontario), doing litigation on behalf of people who have been judged mentally incapable.

Carla McKague

I got into the movement in 1977. I was a first-year law student at the time. A number of years before, in 1963, I'd been through the experience of being hospitalized for psychiatric reasons, undergoing ECT (electroshock), and not having an awfully good time of it. I'd sort of put it away and hadn't thought about it a lot. But some things happened in 1977 that very forcibly brought that time back to my attention.

Just a couple of months into law school, my marriage went up in flames. It was a very awful time and it put me back into the same kind of state of suicidal depression that had got me hospitalized fourteen years earlier. So I was going through my own private hell, dealing with this really terrible situation.

Purely by chance, when I'd started law school I had agreed to spend a couple of days a week working in a student legal-aid clinic and had ended up at the one that was stationed in the Queen Street Mental Health Centre. So I was looking around me at people who were currently hospitalized. And I was just appalled. I was thinking, "It's fourteen years later, and things haven't changed. Things are just as bad as they were back in 1963."

And then, in connection with one of my clients at Queen Street, I met Don Weitz. Just a month or two before, Don had started a group in Toronto, which eventually became On Our Own. Don got me interested and I started going to meetings, and meeting other people who had made their way through the system. Among them were people who actually had a political analysis, who made me look at things in a new way and helped me understand, through their experiences, what some of the problems were.

For example, I had had ECT and had bad after-effects from it. But it had never occurred to me that this was a pattern. I thought I'd just been unlucky. But then I started meeting other people who'd had ECT and who had had similar experiences, many of them far worse than my own. So I started looking into the facts. To make a long story short, I became very active in On Our Own. I'd gone into law school knowing I wanted to work in the area of law and medicine, and it rapidly narrowed down to the area of law and mental health.

I was on the board of Houselink Community Homes, which was providing housing for people coming out of hospital. I helped found the Advocacy Resource Centre for the Handicapped and then worked there, first as an articling student and later for seven years as head of litigation, doing test-case work for people with disabilities. The bulk of what I was doing was mental health-related work.

At first, I was a very active member of, and spokesperson for, the Coalition to Stop Electroshock. But I ended up pulling back from that because of the fact that shortly after the Coalition had gotten going, a major electroshock case came along that I ended up being counsel on. So it was difficult for me to be out expressing my personal views while I was arguing the case in court.

The Mrs. T. case

My client was a young woman. There was a publication ban on her name, so she's known to the legal world only as "Mrs. T." Shortly after being admitted to Hamilton Psychiatric Hospital, she was asked to consent to ECT. She said no. The fact that they asked her, by the way, meant that they thought she was competent to consent.

When she refused, they went to her family for permission. One after another, her husband, her father and her brother refused. And then they went to the Mental Health Review Board and sought an order authorizing them to administer ECT without consent, as they had a right to do under the law at that time—it was 1982. And the Board made that order.

The family started searching frantically for a lawyer who could do something about this. They were referred to me and I took the case on. They called me on a Friday, and the treatments were due to start the following Tuesday, so there was not a lot of time to get things launched. At that time in Ontario, there was no right of appeal to a court from the decisions of the Review Board. What there was—as there always is with a tribunal—was a much more limited right called the right of judicial review. That means you can't go to the court and say, "We think this court made a mistake and gave the wrong decision"; you can only go if the Board either screwed up its procedure—failed to do something it was supposed to—or if it made a ruling where it had no jurisdiction to do so.

So I brought an application for judicial review. Not on procedural grounds, because they'd done the procedure right. The argument that I brought was that the Board didn't have authority to make an order for ECT, because the statute specifically prohibited the Board from authorizing psychosurgery. And I argued that ECT was psychosurgery, according to the definition in the legislation. It was a procedure that removed, destroyed or interrupted the continuity of histologically normal brain tissue. So my basic argument was that ECT caused brain damage and so fell within the definition of psychosurgery. Therefore the Board could not order it.

The case got an enormous amount of publicity, coast to coast. I've got clippings from Edmonton, Vancouver and Newfoundland. The Ontario Minister of Health stood up in the Legislature and said he was personally pretty upset about people being subjected to this treatment when nobody had consented to it. It became very hot politically. It got heard on an expedited basis in court, five weeks after we brought the application—during which five weeks, by the way, as well as carrying a full case load, we conducted examinations of seven expert witnesses, averaging four to five hours each in length. We acquired voluminous amounts of medical journal articles and other information.

To make a long story short, we lost. The judge ruled that I'd raised some really difficult questions, and that it was clear that nobody had all the answers on this subject, but that the onus of proof was on me to show that ECT was damaging. It wasn't on the doctors to show that it wasn't. I lost because I could not provide proof that the likelihood of ECT causing damage was greater than 50 percent.

On my client's instructions, we brought an application for leave to appeal to the Court of Appeal. Before that application was heard, the Ministry of Health approached us and wanted to settle the matter. And their proposal—which was in my client's best interests, which meant I had to go along with it—was that, if we dropped our application for leave to appeal, they would arrange to have Mrs. T. transferred to another doctor and hospital, where she would not be given ECT.

That was done. We dropped our application. We got Mrs. T. off the hook and the Ministry got what they wanted, which was that that decision stood on the books, legitimizing the Board's right to order ECT.

However, almost immediately, the government proclaimed some sections of the Mental Health Act (MHA) that had been passed in 1978, four years earlier, but never proclaimed. These provided a lot more process at Review Board hearings and gave a right of appeal from the Review Board to the court. And the ECT Review Committee was established. I became a member a couple of months after that committee started deliberating. It produced a report that was considerably better than one might have expected. It didn't say ECT shouldn't be used— though it did register that there was one dissenter in that, which was me. It proposed a very elaborate and careful scheme of substitute decision making, which is now part of Ontario law. And it stated very strongly that unless all of the recommendations in that report were followed, there was a strong case for banning ECT in Ontario.

Many of the recommendations have not been followed. The topic more or less went into abeyance until about 1986, when a remarkable thing happened. There was a bill before the legislature at that time because the Charter of Rights and Freedoms had been proclaimed. All of a sudden people had realized that there were all kinds of pieces of legislation in Ontario that didn't conform to the Charter. So they created this bill to patch everything up.

In its original form, Bill 7 had two or three proposed amendments to the MHA. There was one proposal that we quite liked, which was that, for the first time, if your doctor said that you were incompetent, you didn't have to take his word for it. You could go to the Review Board and have his or her decision about your competency reviewed. But other than that, there wasn't much.

A number of us were quite concerned about this. We felt that if the Minister of Health thought this was all that was wrong with the MHA on Charter grounds, then he didn't know his Charter very well. And one Saturday night, I sat down at my computer and drafted another twenty-two proposed amendments to the MHA that would, in my view, make it comply with the Charter. With the backing of a couple of other lawyers and people in the psychiatric survivors' movement, I went and sold them to the opposition.

We had a Liberal government at the time, but it was in the minority. And I sold the amendments to the NDP. What had been anticipated as a half-hour debate on the MHA-related piece of this bill turned into a two-week debate. We'd caught the doctors off guard. They weren't prepared. They went kind of hysterical. So there was a huge battle before the committee studying this bill. When the dust had settled, there had been some very significant changes to the MHA.

However, one we had lost on—narrowly—was attacking the right of the Review Board to make treatment orders. We had said it ought to be good enough that you have a consent from the patient or a substitute consent from someone authorized to give it. If you don't have those, the Board shouldn't be making treatment orders. This was in May. The bill got held up because there was controversy about some other things in it to do with the human rights code—specifically, amendments to prohibit discrimination on the grounds of sexual orientation.

In December, the bill finally got back to the legislature. And when it did, something quite amazing happened. In the interim, the Conservatives, of all unlikely people, had picked up ECT as an issue. They were opposed to forced ECT. So when the bill got back to the House, Evelyn Gigantes of the NDP got up at third reading and, more as a gesture than anything else, reproposed the amendment that would take away the Board's right to make treatment orders. And the Tories got confused and voted for it by mistake. They thought they were voting for an amendment that would forbid the Board's making treatment orders for ECT. They didn't realize they were voting for something that would not allow the Board to make treatment orders at all.

Well, it took them about fifteen minutes to realize their error. They tried to reopen it on the floor of the legislature. That requires all-party consent, and the NDP refused to give consent. All of a sudden, we had a bill that said that the Board couldn't make treatment orders anymore!

Everybody went into shock. The Tories ran off to the Liberal Minister of Health and beat their heads on the ground and said, "We're sorry, we're sorry, how can we fix this?" The Minister laughed a lot because he'd already had the doctors mad at him—the Liberals were pushing through legislation banning extra billing. And now the doctors were going to have somebody else to be mad at—the Tories.

But finally they struck a deal: they would put another section into the bill, delaying proclamation of this particular section until April 1—a most appropriate date, I thought—and meanwhile, they were going to introduce another bill to repeal the amendment. So they brought forth another bill. Counsel to the Ministry of Health, however, persuaded them that, if they were going to give the Board back the right to make treatment orders, there would have to be something to sweeten the package—and proposed what was basically the substitute consent scheme drawn from the recommendations of the ECT Review Committee, which would put in place a much, much better plan for substitute decision making than what currently existed. They figured the doctors would be happy that the Board got the power back, and the patients would be happy to have this wonderful new consent scheme. How it ended up, of course, was that everybody was angry. The doctors hated the consent scheme and the patients hated the Board being able to make treatment orders.

April 1 was approaching, and the bill hadn't even got to Committee yet because Committee was bogged down with other things. So they introduced another bill, which delayed proclamation of the amendment until the end of May.

So now the end of May was approaching, and the Committee was looking at this issue but was by no means ready to make a decision on it. The Minister decided to introduce yet another bill, which would delay proclamation until the following January. Along the way, it had occurred to the Minister that, if competent patients were going to be able to refuse treatment, it would be a good idea if we knew how to figure out who's competent. Consequently, he wanted to delay until the following January so that he could set up a committee to study how one decided who was competent. But there was a slip-up in the Minister's office, and that bill did not get on the order paper.

Come the end of May, the amendment popped into place. Boards no longer had any authority to make treatment orders. All hell broke loose. There was panic in the streets. And a deal was struck within forty-eight hours. Everybody got something out of the deal. What the NDP got was that Review Boards could no longer override the wishes of competent patients. What the Liberals got was that Review Boards could still override decisions made by the appointed substitutes of incompetent patients. And what the Tories got was that Review Boards couldn't order ECT anymore. So we have the Conservative Party of Ontario to thank for that amendment.

More about electroshock

Only about 15 percent of psychiatrists use ECT. But they tend to use it a lot. And they tend to believe that it's the greatest thing since sliced bread and poses no risks. That's what they tell their patients. Well, if you're told about this wonderful miracle cure with no risks, of course you're going to consent to it. Why not?

That's what I'd done. In fact, I actually consented without knowing very much of anything. I was horribly depressed, and the doctor said, "We've got something that will fix you up just fine." And I was never awfully clear about what was actually happening to me when I was unconscious.

The government has been trying for almost ten years now to develop an information package that is acceptable both to the psychiatrists and to the psychiatric survivors' movement. They have, predictably, failed. My own view is that rather than trying to come up with something that everybody can live with, the Ministry should produce a pamphlet that tells both sides of the story: "Here's what the doctors say, and here's what the patients say." And let people make up their own minds.

I should mention that ECT is given to women two and a half to three times as often as it is to men. And the standard explanation is that women are depressed that much more often than men. This is quite true because women have a lot more to be depressed about. But there are a couple of studies around that indicate that even if you're looking at a primary diagnosis not of depression but of, say, schizophrenia, women are still given ECT that much more often. Older women are especially likely to be given ECT.

Ken Gallagher and George Reed both had long psychiatric histories; they'd been "revolving-door" patients for a number of years—in and out of hospital. Both of them, at the time I was dealing with them, were being held not as civilly committed patients, but on Warrants of the Lieutenant Governor (WLG).

The WLG no longer exists; it has a different name now. But before amendments to the Criminal Code, if a person was found either unfit to stand trial or not guilty by reason of insanity, the Lieutenant Governor issued a document called a warrant, which allowed the person to be held "at the pleasure of Her Majesty" in a psychiatric facility. The person was reviewed on an annual basis, and when it was concluded that he (most people put on warrants were men) had recovered from his mental disorder to the point at which it was "in his best interest, and also not contrary to the interests of society" for him to be released, he could be freed.

In Ontario, at that time, the chair of the Board in Ontario was a retired judge of the Ontario Supreme Court named Edson Haines, who had extreme difficulty releasing anybody. He interpreted that test as meaning that you had to show that you had completely recovered from any mental disorder—including your depression at being locked up.

The average length of a warrant in Ontario in those days was eight years, whereas in Quebec, for example, it was three years. In many cases, people's sentences would have been shorter if they'd been tried and found guilty. In some cases, sentences would have been longer. The crimes people were accused of ranged from badly bungled amateur bank robberies to murder.

Ken and George had both been found not guilty, by reason of insanity, of criminal offences. They were being held in Oak Ridge, which is the maximum-security facility at the Penetanguishene Mental Health Centre [located in rural Ontario].

Oak Ridge is an old, old building. It's a prison, not a hospital. Its staff are hired for their brawn rather than for their brains. It has no programs that anybody would call effective therapy. In fact, Russell Fleming, who was at that time administrator of the Ridge and is now administrator of the entire mental health centre, has been on national television saying that you don't do people any favour by sending them there. The programs are nonexistent. Drug therapy is where it's at. They do have workshops, but the workshops are dull and mind-numbing. The mentality of the staff is a prison mentality. They don't think of themselves as nurses; they think of themselves as guards.

My particular horror in the place is the admission ward, where people are housed when they first arrive, often for a thirty- or sixty-day psychiatric assessment. Each inmate lives in a barren cell with a toilet built into the wall (so that he can't tear it out). He is given a mattress made of quilted canvas (so that he can't tear it up and hang himself with the strips), a hospital gown of quilted canvas, and nothing else. He spends twenty-three out of every twenty-four hours in this cell. He is taken out for one hour each day, for psychological testing. You can imagine the results of psychological testing after twenty-three hours in such a cell.

Oak Ridge is a terrible, terrible place.

This is where my clients were; not on the admission ward, but on other wards. They had been reviewed annually to assess their potential for release. One of them had been there for six years, the other for eight. In each case, there was a long preceding psychiatric history.

Ken and George had a couple of things in common. They were both diagnosed as chronic paranoid schizophrenics. The general consensus was that neither of them was ever going to return to society. If they made sufficient progress, they might get out of maximum security into medium security, but there wasn't much hope of their ever progressing further than that.

The other thing they had in common was that neither of them wanted neuroleptic drugs. They had been on and off them over the years. I can't say they'd never consented. A couple of times they had, in situations such as being told, "George, we will let you out of seclusion if you will take your drugs." But more often they had been treated either with the substitute consent of a family member or according to an order of the Review Board.

And first one and then the other came to me through the Patient Advocate and said, "Make them stop. We don't want these drugs anymore. We've been drugged and we've been crazy, and we would rather be crazy." And I agreed to take on this fight.

There were actually two rounds to the fight. The first time that we went up the line, I was using a technical argument based on the wording of the MHA. I was arguing that with patients held under a WLG, the Board had no authority to make a treatment order. Two days before we were due to be in the Court of Appeal on this first round, the Ministry of Health changed the law, which mooted the whole thing, so we were back to square one.

When we started the second round, I brought a challenge to the MHA itself. I argued that it was not in accordance with the Charter that a Board be able to make an order authorizing treatment that the person had refused when competent. It was accepted that there were periods at which my clients had been competent, during which they had refused the treatment. There was no quarrel about that. But the position of the hospital and the Ministry was that this was not the appropriate test; the appropriate test was what was in their best interests, as defined by the MHA.

The MHA included tests of whether the treatment was likely to substantially improve their mental condition, whether lack of treatment would not, whether less intrusive or restrictive measures could be taken and so on. But it did not include anything about people's wishes when competent.

My argument was that substitute decision makers (SDMs), for example, when they knew the person's competent wishes, were bound to abide by those wishes. In the case of both my clients, the official SDM was Ontario's Official Guardian—family had opted out.

When they had refused the treatment, my clients had been declared incompetent. The Official Guardian had been brought in and after investigation had said, "Both of these people, when competent, had expressed wishes not to have this treatment, and therefore we will not consent." That's the point at which it went to the Board. And at that point the Board had authority to override substitutes.

And I said, "Wait a minute. The whole Act, at this point, says that competent wishes matter. Substitutes have to abide by competent wishes; that's their first criterion. But when you get to the Board, that's not a criterion at all. The Board isn't even allowed to look at what their competent wishes were; it's not part of the test. And this violates Section 7 of the Charter, which deals with security of the person, among other things. And it violates Section 15, which is the equality section. The only people in Ontario who can be treated against their will are involuntary psychiatric patients."

I lost both George's and Ken's Board hearings, which took three and four days, respectively. The cases were appealed to what was then the Ontario District Court. The only thing the judge agreed with was that I had a right to make Charter arguments to the Board. But then he said that all my arguments stank.

We appealed from there to the Court of Appeal—with all kind of delays, by the way. The original Board hearings were in 1987 and we got to the Court of Appeal in 1991. We argued before them for three days. And the Court of Appeal said, "You're right. They can't do this. And we are in fact striking out this part of the MHA as being in violation of the Charter. We're still going to let the Review Boards override substitutes where the substitute has made a best-interests call and the Board disagrees, but we're no longer going to let them override when substitutes are acting on the wishes that people expressed when they were capable." [As of April 1995, they have not been able to override substitutes who make best-interests decisions either.]

The court, to my great pleasure, included in its decision three or four paragraphs describing the dangers of neuroleptic drugs. I had put in some submissions, partly from medical literature and partly from a couple of important cases in the United States (the *Rogers* cases, out of the State of Massachusetts, and *Re: Guardianship of Richard Roe*).

In fact, when this decision came down, I got the signal honour of being accorded the "Quote of the Day" in the *Globe and Mail*. And the line they chose to quote was my statement, which went something like, "What this case stands for is the proposition that people are entitled to choose their own hell." If you've experienced psychosis or whatever one wants to call it and you've experienced the medications and they're both awful, you have the right to choose which awful thing you want. And my clients both opted for psychosis.

In practice, this ruling has not made much difference in psychiatric patients' lives. One of the problems we have is that doctors do not inform patients about the risks of medication. The law requires that they do so. But I must tell you that in all my years of working in this field, I can count on the fingers of one hand the number of clients I've had whose doctors have informed them about tardive dyskinesia, for example.

Back in 1980, there was an inquest into the death of a young man named Aldo Alviani, who was given something like twenty times the recommended maximum dose of neuroleptics and then had it topped off with fifty milligrams of intravenous Valium. There was a little coalition that was formed in connection with that inquest, and we did a survey. We're not pretending it's a scientific survey. We went out and grabbed the first hundred people we could find who had been psychiatrically hospitalized in the preceding two years, and we asked them what they'd been told about proposed treatments, whether drugs or ECT. We found that almost nobody was told about the dangers. At best, they would be told, "Your vision will be blurred," or "You're going to twitch." We also found, much more surprisingly, that 80 percent of them had not been told anything about the beneficial effects of the drugs. At most, they were told generalities like, "This will make the voices go away." The amount of information people were given was almost nil. And this is still the case now.

There was an interesting article written by a doctor who was, at that time, the person in charge of education at the Queen Street Mental Health Centre. He now runs the sole provincial psychiatric institution in Nova Scotia. He published an article in a journal called *Health Law in Canada*, entitled "Informed Consent in Psychiatric Settings." The basic message was this: If you get a patient admitted to a psychiatric hospital, don't tell him the truth about treatment. Because if you do, he'll refuse.

Mental Health Acts

The Ontario standard for admitting people to a psychiatric facility against their will is that they, as a result of a mental disorder, must present a risk of serious harm to themselves, such as suicide or self-mutilation; or they must present a risk of serious physical harm to someone else; or they must be so incapable of caring for themselves that they are at risk of imminent and serious physical impairment. Currently, a person may only be given psychiatric treatment with either personal consent, if competent, or a valid substitute consent, if incompetent. In British Columbia, the moment you become an involuntary psychiatric patient, all treatment decisions are made by the administrator of the facility. There is not even an inquiry into whether you're capable of making your own decisions. In the Yukon, you can be civilly committed for damaging property—even your own property!

I don't understand why societies see the need for special laws dealing with people who are perceived as having mental disorders. We do not have a Cancer Act or an Epilepsy Act. If anybody proposed that we should have ways of forcing hospitalization and treatment on people who have cancer, I think there would be a huge public outcry. But the perception is that somehow things that happen in your mind are different.

Furthermore, the protections entrenched in the MHA are not enforced. Psychiatrists routinely do things that are illegal. It happens daily in virtually every hospital with a psychiatric ward in this province. Doctors are quite unwilling to learn what the law is. I had the experience last year of going on tour with the Ontario Hospital Association, which held seminars in six cities to tell people about impending changes in the legislation around consent to treatment—not just psychiatric treatment, but medical treatment in general. And almost without exception, no doctors attended. Nurses attended. Record-keepers and administrators attended. But doctors were conspicuous by their absence.

Psychiatrists' unjustified arrogance

We're in a period of profound societal change in all kinds of ways. And one of the most important ways is that doctors are being dragged off their pedestals. Doctors have historically believed that MD stands for Medical Deity. That their judgements are not to be questioned. And institutional psychiatrists have been supported in this belief by laws that give them immense power over people's lives.

Some doctors in every branch of medicine have always had this "doctor knows best" attitude and the feeling that they can just go ahead and do what they feel is necessary, whether the patients really understand what's happening or not. But psychiatrists are the only ones who've had that supported by law. We, as a society, have officially given them some very significant powers. And they are resisting like crazy being dragged into what is almost the twenty-first century.

For example, a particular doctor, whom I won't name, was one of the people consulted about the recommendations of the ECT Review Committee. The Ministry held a meeting to say, "Here are the recommendations, and here's what we intend to do about it." Leaving the meeting, he turned to one of the Ministry people and said, "You can pass whatever laws you like; we're still going to do whatever we want."

There's a tendency to see psychiatrists as expert, even in areas in which they're not expert. There's a book which I would recommend to anyone interested in this area by a man named Jonas Robicher, who was both a psychiatrist and a lawyer, called *The Powers of Psychiatry*. Robicher doesn't question the traditional role of psychiatry, which is, in his view, to heal the sick. But he's very concerned about the expansion of that role. He doesn't see why we should use psychiatrists to decide who we should hire, or who should get the kids, or what was really going on with Napoleon.

Pathologizing odd behaviour

Society has an enormously stereotypical view of the crazy person, who is seen as a kind of cross between an incompetent six-year-old child and Jack the Ripper. People are scared of crazy people. People don't want them around, because they don't know what they're going to do next. In fact, some studies have shown that the incidence of violence among people with a psychiatric label is as much as seven times lower than among other people. The typical person who's been labelled schizophrenic is an enormously passive individual who's never going to hurt anybody. But some people with that label do hurt other people, and a few have done so in spectacularly bizarre ways. And then everybody gets tarred with the same brush.

Sociologist Erving Goffman, in his book *Stigma*, talks about the fact that we have, as a society, expectations of how people are going to behave. We don't, for example, expect someone to walk into a fancy restaurant and start taking their clothes off. When people violate the norms of societal behaviour, we're taken aback. And one of the ways that we deal with it is by pathologizing that behaviour. Instead of saying, "Here's someone who's done something I didn't expect," we say, "Here's someone who must be sick because he's done something I didn't expect."

We don't live comfortably with uncertainty. We want to know what the guy in the next office or the person at the next table in the restaurant is likely to do. And we get really uneasy when that person violates our expectations. Because we're uneasy with that, we pathologize it. Once we've pathologized it, we have the expectation that because the person is unpredictable, this may lead to, at the least, embarrassment, and, at the worst, violence. We want someone to do something about it. We don't want unpredictable people in our lives. And therefore we say, "Let's take these unpredictable people and put them somewhere where they can be made predictable, or, if they can't, at least we don't have to cope with them anymore."

My present view is that mental illness probably doesn't exist. I'm willing to be persuaded otherwise, given proof. I haven't yet seen any. I am not persuaded by any of the current genetic and biochemical studies. Yes, there are biochemical effects of the problems that people have. Yes, if you get depressed, certain things happen to your brain that are measurable and palpable. But those, in my view, are effects rather than causes. I have an awful lot of trouble with the whole idea of the current vogue in psychiatry, which is to define everything as chemical and say, "We don't need to talk to them; we just need to give them pills."

"Partnership" and coercion

I would like to see the movement totally disavow the official CMHA model, which is a partnership model that sees the patient, the family and the care provider jointly deciding what happens to people. The inevitable outcome of this model is that the patient becomes the silent partner. The minute you get joint decision making, the patient is disempowered.

It sounds terrific; it sounds like we're all going to work together in harmony and everything's going to come out so everybody's happy. But it doesn't work. What you get is a decision made by families and care providers, and the patient is cowed into assenting to it. This is not a partnership. To go back to my earlier analogy, nobody would propose a partnership between the cancer patient, the patient's family and the doctor. The cancer patient is in control. The cancer patient decides to have chemotherapy or radiation, or not to. I think this is really a central question and that any suggestion of partnership should be immediately shunned.

What we really need is to get rid of institutionalization and to have community alternatives that work because psychiatric survivors are involved in their design, implementation and operation. We need nonthreatening alternatives; things that people will come to by choice because they find them helpful.

Coercive treatment simply does not work. You drag people in and you forcibly medicate them and subject them to coercive measures, and this alienates them from the system designed to help them. You get them saying, "I will never go back to that place, because of what they did to me."

What we need to do, I think, is remove the element of coercion. We need to have things available to people who are struggling, people who are in anguish, people who want help. And we have to avoid imposing on the person what we think is good for them. The only one who is entitled to decide what's good for a person is that person.

I want to end with a little anecdote: A number of years ago, a friend of mine reported attending a session at the Clarke Institute of Psychiatry [Toronto's prestigious research facility and teaching hospital] designed for a group called Friends and Relatives of the Mentally Ill, which is a sort of analogue to Friends of Schizophrenics [which has since changed its name to the Schizophrenia Society]. One of the friends and relatives in the audience got up and confronted one of the doctors, saying, "Why is it so hard to get our family members into hospital? Why can't you take them in and treat them?" And the doctor's response was, "Well, we used to be able to do that, but now, when we do, *Phoenix Rising* gets on our back."

"Losing it" in Banff

At the Banff conference where Carla McKague and I put on a workshop together, *Phoenix Rising* was supposed to be my topic. But instead, I spoke about myself, and about psychiatry, and about drugs. I talked about the fact that it was legal to force people to take horrendous drugs like Haldol, but illegal for people to voluntarily take drugs like marijuana and LSD. I said these were infinitely less harmful than psychiatric drugs and could actually make people feel good. I remember Ryan telling me afterwards that she'd heard a gaggle of scandalized feminist therapists in the elevator complaining that one of the speakers at the conference was promoting street drugs. I was delighted.

Unfortunately, however, I went crazy at this conference. For one thing, being surrounded by hundreds of mental health professionals was very frightening. And then, I'd had a couple of sleepless nights before the conference started.

Ryan, who had come with me, was taking Ritalin at the time. Her psychiatrist prescribed it for her. Ritalin is routinely given to children labelled hyperactive. It's an amphetamine that is mysteriously supposed to calm difficult children, and is not generally given to adults, as it makes them speedy. But Ryan was an exceedingly odd person and she told me Ritalin made her stop hallucinating, and nothing else did. I had gotten Ritalin from her a couple of times before to stay awake at work after being up all night. And at this conference, I was taking it every day. I didn't sleep the whole time.

I was also under enormous stress from the possibility that I'd get the CMHA job. I got out of bed about 3 a.m. on the last night of the conference and went outside with my tape recorder, which I'd brought with me to interview people for "Analyzing Psychiatry," a radio program I was putting together for the CBC "Ideas" series (which was broadcast in April 1990; another program I did, "By Reason of Insanity," was broadcast in November 1991. The huge flood of letters from all over Canada responding to the first show, in particular, confirmed for me how many people are concerned about psychiatry). I had thought I could get some mental health professionals at this conference to incriminate themselves on tape. But I never did. I went nuts instead. I went outside with the tape recorder and sat on this beautiful, grassy slope in the dark, sobbing into the microphone about how I wasn't going to be able to work for the CMHA—that it would kill me to try. And I went on at myself about being bad.

Meanwhile, the Alberta representative of the CMHA's national "consumer" network had been slated to facilitate the consumer caucus, where we were supposed to come up with recommendations to the conference, and then represent consumers at the closing plenary session. But she'd been feeling like she couldn't handle it, and had asked me a couple of days earlier if I would take over for her. "Sure, no problem," I'd burbled, high as a kite on coffee and Ritalin.

This major task was completely unrelated to what I was supposed to be doing. I'd also made an appointment to interview Jeffrey Masson that morning. I was sleepless and excited and high and stressed out. Scary faces started forming and changing before my eyes. Outlines were too sharp, colours painfully bright. One false move on my part would result in unspeakable peril. Someone was out to get me, and I didn't know who or why. The only way out was to kill myself.

After I went back to bed around 4 a.m., I started talking to Ryan about my impending suicide. I demanded a lot of attention from her that night, and she was generous with her time and caring. But when I finally let her go to sleep, I was still in the land of extreme strangeness.

At 6 a.m. I phoned Masson and cancelled our interview. Then I phoned a woman psychiatrist with whom I'd booked another interview and said, "I talked to you yesterday. I'm the one doing a show for the CBC. And I'm crazy, right at this very moment. Can I come talk to you?" She replied, "No, I'm afraid I'm busy." I was lucky. If she'd agreed to see me, I probably would have landed on some back ward in an Alberta mental hospital, completely dysfunctional on psychiatric drugs.

By 7 a.m. I was staggering around one of the sumptuous lobbies of the Banff Springs Hotel, going up to mental health professionals and saying, "Hi, I'm having a psychotic episode. Can you help me?" Fortunately, they all ignored me. I called the Alberta woman and told her I couldn't facilitate anything that day, as I'd gone out of my mind. She said not to worry—she'd slept well for a couple of nights believing she was off the hook, and now felt relaxed enough to manage.

Then I went back to the room, and Ryan (who is a saint) gave me a bubble bath and then very gently told me that I should lie down and close my eyes, even if I couldn't sleep, because I needed rest. She held me and talked to me, humorously and kindly. She kept telling me I was going to be okay. I cried quite a bit. By the time the final plenary was on, I'd stopped being crazy and just felt very, very tired. But I attended it anyway and went up to the mike and said, "I know I've been a squeaky wheel at this conference, but I'm asking you to invite me back to the next conference anyway." They did, and the following year I had the opportunity to hear Kate Millett, author of *The Loony Bin Trip*, say what she thought about psychiatry. She was inspiring.

I thought it was interesting that the first and second times I went mad, I got professional help—hospitalization and drugs—and stayed crazy for months, and the third time I got help from a friend who wasn't scared because she'd been there herself—and it was over in a few hours.

Leash law

In that same year, 1989, I was asked to speak at an event at PARC—the Parkdale Activity and Recreation Centre. PARC was a drop-in, mostly for people who'd been discharged from the Queen Street Mental Health Centre. Parkdale is a psychiatric ghetto, full of heavily medicated people living in hideous boarding homes. The event was about a proposed "leash law." Ontario was planning to pass legislation whereby, if you didn't comply with your treatment plan—that is, see your psychiatrist and take your drugs— after you got out of hospital, the mental health establishment could jerk your leash, so to speak, and lock you up again.

The government was about to hold public hearings on the leash law, and this forum was to let crazy people know why they should go to these hearings and tell the politicians that the law was unacceptable. I told my own story and talked about how hideous it would be if this law were passed.

The leash-law forum was where I first met Randy Pritchard. He wasn't one of the official speakers, but he got up after the rest of us had spoken and told the crowd that he was on a Warrant of the Lieutenant Governor, having been found not guilty of a crime by reason of insanity. He spoke very persuasively and movingly about his situation. Many years earlier, he had become involved in a plot to assassinate the prime minister after martial law was declared in Canada. He'd been caught in Ottawa with the key to a locker that had explosives in it. He'd wanted to plead guilty but his lawyer persuaded him to plead not guilty by reason of insanity. He did time first in Oak Ridge, and then on the forensic (criminal) unit at the Clarke Institute of Psychiatry. He described what life on a WLG was like and said that if we let this law go through, we'd all be in the same kind of trouble he was in— if we looked at somebody sideways we could get locked up again.

I was very impressed with Randy. He came up to me when the event was over and asked what I, as editor of *Phoenix Rising*, could do to help the human rights group he'd started for forensic patients (those involved in the criminal aspect of psychiatry) and their families. I told him the magazine was on its way out and that I doubted I could do anything much for his group. He told me that he didn't agree with my antipsychiatry stance completely, though he thought I had some good points.

One of the people who put together the leash-law forum was David Reville. David's experience in psychiatric hospitals led him into community activism, which eventually led to what he calls Big P Politics. During terms as Toronto City Councillor, Member of Provincial Parliament for a downtown Toronto riding and Special Advisor to the Premier (back when Ontario had an NDP government), he not only remembered where he'd come from but spoke about it often, in order to keep crazy people's issues on the agenda.

O

David Reville

I met Don Weitz soon after I came to Toronto, in the 1970s. He was meeting with a bunch of crazies who at that time called themselves the Ontario Mental Patients Association, which later became On Our Own. That was my first experience with self-help, which was what got me started in understanding that if you work together, you can support one another and feel better about yourself. And maybe, if you stay together long enough and figure out what's going on, you can make some changes.

One of my first big national things, as a survivor, came out of the Ken Kesey movie *One Flew Over the Cuckoo's Nest*. CTV wanted to do a show about whether that movie was realistic. They were looking for a crazy, but they couldn't find one. Most people wouldn't admit it; most people were trying to pass for normal. But they found me.

When I was quite young, this nice shrink had told me I was incurably mentally ill. Then I went into the Big House in Kingston [Kingston Psychiatric Hospital, a provincial facility]. I felt it was intolerable. I started to write about how horrible it was, and I decided to smuggle my work out. [David's story was eventually published in *Phoenix Rising*.]

Anyway, CTV wanted me to go on Canada AM to say whether the scenario in

One Flew Over the Cuckoo's Nest was possible. Whether it could really happen today. I said, "Of course. I even recognize the people in the film." Whoever did the casting was so good that I felt like I lived with those guys. We didn't have anybody quite as bad as Big Nurse, but we had people who were trying out for the part. It was all so true.

After that happened, all kinds of people began to call me up and say, "You're our team crazy." I then did CBC-FM shows with Don and others, and I started to build my reputation as a guy with the stigma who could talk about it. That started to spread. People who wanted to do something about mental health would call me up and say, "Oh, you're a crazy who can manage in a meeting. Amazing. Your medication must be really well adjusted. I always thought crazy people were stupid, but you're not."

You can be crazy and smart. Crazy does not mean stupid. Lots of people think it does; many of them are psychiatric service providers. I had a big fight with an attendant on the ward. Because I was crazy, he refused to believe that I had a university education. Granted, most of us didn't, because we'd been struck down too soon. He said to me, "Wait a minute; irregardless of the fact that you've been in university—" and I said, "Irregardless is not a word."

I've been doing this for twenty-seven years. During the first several years, there were hardly any of us. We were worn out, bummed out, burned out. Now there's all sorts of action. New leaders are coming forward. People in little tiny towns are saying, "Yeah, I'm crazy; yeah, I want to join this group; yeah, I want to feel better about my experience; yeah, I want to do something." I am so excited about seeing crazy people taking power, making our movement grow. Everywhere I go in Canada, I can see it happening. It happens in different ways in different places, of course, as it should. But it's happening from the Yukon to Newfoundland. We're starting to find some people who are prepared to listen to what we're saying. The trick is to keep it all going. We need not only to have more people involved, but also to have them doing more kinds of things, wherever they're located and whatever they care about. Because we care about all kinds of things.

One of the things I'm most excited about is the seven or eight survivor businesses that have started in Ontario. I think that's the frontier for us, where crazies have their own work, run by crazies. Where you have real work to do and you get all the benefits of that. You're paid real money and you're expected to do the job. It's not like some sheltered workshop, where you're paid a few pennies per hour and nobody really cares whether you put the washers in the bag. You have a real job; working conditions meet your needs, and you deliver what you can deliver. You get a pay cheque and you know you've earned that money.

I feel quite guilty about the quality of my survival. I own my own house. My life is quite different from those of most survivors. My connection is that I do know how it feels to be pushed around. And that I'm still afraid. Not about being crazy, but about what they'll do to me if they catch me again. My craziness is my problem, and I can cope fine with that. I have my own strategies for it. I'm just worried about being in four-point restraints [tied up by the wrists and ankles]; being locked up and shot up and fucked up.

I think that my psychiatric experience has hurt me in ways that I'll never get over. I'll always feel damaged by the way society has responded to my label. But if somebody came along and "fixed" me, I wouldn't be myself anymore. And that would be a problem for me, because all that stuff is part of who I am. Part of who I am is having been on the violent ward, where I was horrified, but I also learned a lot. I wouldn't give up that experience for the world, because I learned so much about power relations. And otherwise I probably wouldn't have believed that things like that could happen. I was a nice, middle-class kid.

○

Our Turn

Shortly after the leash-law forum, Hugh Tapping (who had previously recommended that I try for the CMHA job) asked me to join a committee called the People Unlabelled Network (PUN), whose purpose was to choose people from Ontario who would be subsidized to attend Our Turn, the first ever national conference for crazy people in Canada. Our Turn took place in Montreal, in November 1989, and was set up by the Regroupement de ressources alternatives en santé mentale du Québec [the Coalition of Alternative Mental Health Resources of Quebec], with support from the CMHA. But the CMHA had very little presence at it.

Hugh Tapping had the task of finding Ontarians to attend this national conference. He invited me and four others to form PUN, so that he wouldn't have to choose people on his own, arbitrarily. PUN wrote to all the CMHA drop-ins and other appropriate places, announcing the conference and saying, "If you want to attend, write and tell us why." We received hundreds of letters from people all over the province, and chose the people who we felt would both get the most out of the conference and bring the most to it.

Former and current mental patients of all political stripes came to Our Turn from all over Canada. It was invigorating to be at a conference with a couple of hundred other people who'd been locked up and gotten out and were willing to talk about it. Who were proud of having lived through it.

I presented one half of a debate on the pros and cons of psychiatric drugs. The man who was defending the drugs was very sweet and gentle; it was not at all a hostile debate.

One of the best events was a performance by the Puzzle Factory, a theatre troupe for psychiatric survivors, founded by L.E. Roze. The show, directed by activist Linda Carter, was called *Brain Forest, or How Do You Slam a Revolving Door?* It was an awesome musical, alternately hilarious and deeply moving. In one piece, a woman walked around with a big box over her head, open at the front so you could see her face, and talked to the audience from inside this box. There were bits about medications, social work and so on. There was a maniacal doctor doling out multicoloured pills to everyone. At the end there was a wedding in which the bride was a tall, bearded man in a fabulous gown and the groom was a woman in a tux. Then the actors invited people from the audience to dance with them on the stage.

Two of the speakers at Our Turn were Louise Pembroke, spokesperson of Survivors Speak Out, a radical organization in London, England; and Judi Chamberlin, author of *On Our Own: Patient-Controlled Alternatives to the Mental Health System* and one of the founding members of the U.S. mad movement. Judi talked about the survivor-run advocacy centre she helped found; Louise spoke about the need for "rage rooms"—safe, soundproof places where people can scream, hit things and express their rage, rather than having it suppressed by drugs. I'll never forget Louise's description of being held down on the floor by two nurses while another gave her a needle in the ass. She thought, "One day, I'm going to tell people about this." I think we all wanted to cry when she said that, and at the same time wanted to jump up and down and cheer.

Judi and Louise both spoke about the term "psychiatric survivor" and how they'd been labelled "consumers." Louise had felt much more "consumed" than "consuming" in her relationship with psychiatry. Judi talked about why the word "survivor" was used in the States, where there is a national consumer organization as well as a national psychiatric survivor organization.

She spoke of our strength in having survived psychiatric treatment. At the end of the conference we voted on what we should call ourselves, and the majority voted for the term "psychiatric survivors." For many, Our Turn was the first contact they'd had with the mad movement. People spoke about it for years afterwards with gratitude and amazement.

The Regroupement de ressources alternatives—the group that put on Our Turn—is one of two coalitions dealing with psychiatric patients' issues in Quebec. The other is AGIDD—Association des groupes d'intervention en défense des droits en santé mentale du Québec, or the Association of Mental Health Rights Advocacy Groups of Quebec. Paul Morin helped found the first mental patients' rights group in Montreal, which was the precursor of AGIDD. Paul worked with psychologist David Cohen on *Guide critique des médicaments de l'âme* (*A Critical Guide to Psychotropic Drugs*). He has also collaborated with David on other research projects in the area of psychiatry. Although he is not a psychiatric survivor himself, he has tried his best to change the psychiatric system. He has a Ph.D. in sociology and currently coordinates a community group; he hopes to contribute to the movement in part by developing networking between community groups and the academic field.

○

Paul Morin

In 1976 I spent four months in Europe, and came across the movement to close psychiatric hospitals in Italy. One of my uncles had been psychiatrized. As someone who became politically aware in the 1960s, I've always been interested in the question of normality. I have a degree in sociology and another in communications.

I think it's a question of sensibility. If you question the concept of normality and you are interested in human rights, you want to confront psychiatry.

My involvement with the movement began about 1980. I met with other people in Quebec City, some of whom had been psychiatrized, including a good friend of mine. We founded the first patients' rights group in Quebec. At the beginning of the 1980s, there was an embryonic alternatives movement in Quebec; some self-help groups, some therapeutic communities. Some were led by psychiatrized people.

At the beginning, we were about eight or ten people. We focussed mostly on what we considered to be the law that most needed changing—the public guardianship law. Under this law, if a psychiatrist found that you were incapable of looking after your money, it was impossible for you to refuse treatment. The guardianship law was an easy target, because it clearly didn't make sense.

The public curator was a bad administrator, so we were able to focus on the administrative aspect. We made an impact in the media and quite rapidly established our expertise in that field. And we made a ninety-minute video with testimonies by psychiatrized people, including one of the "guinea pigs" of the Cameron experiments. We showed that video, which promoted the abolition of psychiatry in Quebec, all over the province. It was distributed by a group called Video Femmes in Quebec City.

The group we started was called AutoPsy, and there were other AutoPsys in Shawinigan and Montreal. AGIDD came out of AutoPsy. Quebec has two federations. One is AGIDD, the human-rights coalition, and the other is the Regroupement des ressources alternatives en santé mentale du Québec, which is focussed on developing alternatives (self-help, crisis centres, housing, etc.). Right now there are thirty-six groups in AGIDD and almost a hundred in the Regroupement. We were the first group focussed on rights. There were already some self-help groups and some focussed on housing.

Solidarité Psychiatrie began in 1979. They produced sensitization materials: movies, books and videos. There was also an emphasis on public speaking and on creating alternatives to psychiatry. The group was started by a professional.

I think there are fifty or sixty self-help groups in Quebec now, but there's only one that's controlled by survivors, as far as I know. And there is a split in that group, I heard, between those who are more radical and those who consider themselves "users" of mental health services.

Since 1982 we've had user committees [patient councils] in every psychiatric hospital, by law, but they are not really effective. It's kind of perverse, but the bigger the hospital, the more money the user committee has. Most of the people in hospital have real problems, and it's very hard to organize them. AGIDD doesn't really have enough resources.

Right now we have about fifteen regional advocacy groups whose mandate is to defend and promote the rights of people who have been psychiatrized. Our mandate is not written into law, so we don't have that much power, but people can come to us and ask for help with welfare, or unemployment insurance, or changing their doctor, or if they have problems keeping their children—anything that concerns the question of rights.

I think the question of rights requires the unification of marginalized people. It's a very political thing.

I think if you did a study of the user committees, you'd find that they're not as effective as they should be. And AGIDD cannot really denounce them, because they're part of AGIDD. If AGIDD had more money, there could be a full-time job for someone making sure that the user committees are functioning properly. And if we had more resources, we could get the self-help groups more interested in the question of rights.

We have hired ten psychiatrized people who will be trained to train others to defend themselves. We don't want to take charge of people. Ideally, we'd just like to give out information and get people doing what needs to be done, with the offer of help if they need it. What we want to develop is peer advocacy.

AGIDD's advocacy mandate

AGIDD has a proactive mandate. For instance, there is a new civil code in Quebec, as of January 1, 1994. When two psychiatrists evaluate you as dangerous, a judge must agree with them in order for you to be committed. But you can have a lawyer and be heard by the judge as well.

We have access to these judicial documents in Monteregie, where I work. So we went to the hospital and said "We want to see so-and-so. We know they are being kept against their will." That created a fuss—we've been kicked out of two hospitals because they didn't recognize our proactive mandate, and it is not in the law. We've tried to settle this; we've written to the Department of Mental Health of Quebec. The staff says, "Yes, the collective is right, they have a proactive mandate." But the chief psychiatrist says, "No, we won't answer their questions." So AGIDD will write directly to the Minister and ask whether or not we really have a proactive mandate.

We have some problems going into the hospitals anyway. We can go only when we are called. And people don't necessarily know us. Once we've made ourselves known, people recognize us and ask us for information. But just seeing our poster on the wall doesn't make people call us.

It depends on the government. The lobby group composed of the families of psychiatrized people is pushing really hard for legislation that would make it easier for them to get their relatives incarcerated and forcibly drugged. The balance seems to be tipping away from rights. But we'll see. Psychiatrized people now have the right to be heard by a judge; if, for instance, I'm your father and I want to have a warrant from the judge to commit you, the law says you must be informed. We are doing some research on this.

The problem is, people will be heard by a judge, but the judge will almost always agree with the psychiatrist that the person before him is a dangerous madman.

At best, if you have a very, very good case, you can ask for an interim judgement. The hospital asks to keep you twenty days, and the judge says it should be seven. And you can go to the judge and say, "I'll get another expert." But that's a pretty expensive thing. Getting an expert opinion from a psychiatrist that will be favourable to you can cost six or seven hundred dollars. If you are on welfare, the government will pay that. But the problem is, if you have a minimum-wage job and make six dollars an hour, you are not eligible for assistance.

Alternatives?

Here in Quebec the movement is really an alliance between people who have been psychiatrized and people you could call professional or semiprofessional. The question to be asked is, has that alliance produced a real alternatives movement?

The Regroupement has done a study on people who use its resources, and almost all of them have continued to be involved in psychiatry. If you are having serious emotional problems, there are only the hospitals. There are places you can go if, for instance, your mother just died and you're depressed. They're called psychosocial crisis houses. But the crisis centres are quite selective. They are there to lessen the load on emergency rooms. If you're wild, you're taken to the hospital.

We want to work on peer counselling; we think that's the way of the future. And we want to develop cultural interventions also. We're working with another community group that's well trained in the technique called Theatre of the Oppressed. We've programmed a series of eight performances, and all the actors will be psychiatrized people. But this was not initiated by psychiatrized people.

In groups that belong to AGIDD, the president must be a psychiatrized person, and the board must have a majority of psychiatrized people. There is no such specification in the Regroupement. Half the board must come from a group that says its board has a majority of psychiatrized people. But that doesn't mean the Regroupement representative is likely to have been psychiatrized.

Right now there is a fuss about the question of self-help because most of the self-help groups are not controlled by psychiatrized people. The Regroupement has developed a position paper intended to create debate on this topic. It talks about the difference between self-help and people being helped by others.

Just recently I learned that the ex-coordinator of AGIDD was doing a training session for a self-help group in St-Jean. And the president of the group, who has not been psychiatrized, said, "There's no need to be so precise. We are in mental health, and the people are not that intelligent."

Last year, there was a Regroupement conference. One of the speakers was Daniel Dore, one of the members of Les frères et soeurs d'Emile Nelligan. [This means "The brothers and sisters of Emile Nelligan." Nelligan was a nineteenth-century poet who spent most of his life in a mental hospital in Montreal and died there. Les frères et soeurs is a loose group of fifty people who began as a committee of the Regroupement.] He said "I want to compare the activities of a so-called self-help group with those of another kind of group." He talked about the activities of these two groups. Then he said, "Well, the other group is the child-care centre where my son goes." So, there's really a problem with the self-help movement.

I think the Quebec movement's greatest accomplishment is the fact that the government has finally recognized and focussed on the issue of rights. But it's very difficult because family groups are pushing in the opposite direction. I don't know if this focus will stand very long. But I think it's a good thing.

I've been in the movement for fifteen years, and now we have more leverage and more money. So I think there's progress, and there's more balance. Some psychiatrists are really apprehensive about our group. Perhaps they exaggerate our potential, but they're kind of fearful. That's a good thing. And more psychiatrized people have become involved. That involvement is fragile, but I think it's important.

Les frères et soeurs d'Emile Nelligan

In the early 1980s there was an underground movement in Montreal. It helped people get out of hospital and hide, and it took care of them until they got over their problems. Now that's too dangerous; there is better coordination between mental health and law.

In 1984 there was an event called Polyculture—an international festival of culture and madness. It was put on by AutoPsy. There were many videos and other kinds of art. This was done again in 1987 and in 1990.

Between 1985 and 1989 many self-help groups came together. There were alliances with community workers, some of whom called themselves professionals. Some were on power trips. There were many programs, services and activities. There was an emphasis on housing, social activities and community-oriented programs.

The government's stated wish to be partners with users of mental health services has been a waste of energy. Money has gone to "self-help" and advocacy groups led by professionals, and the power has never been in the hands of psychiatrized people. People have become involved who just wanted things for themselves: money, jobs. They join groups without having any philosophical or personal background in the area. They have good intentions, but often they have stronger personalities than the psychiatrized people and end up having all the power.

The crisis centres created because bureaucrats wanted to lighten the load on hospitals are mini-institutions. People bring their drugs with them. Mostly the centres provide occupation during the day and a social network.

The ideology of alternatives, which had always been important here, fell apart after 1989, when the mental health policy came in. There was a shift to institutional practices. The government causes divisions between groups. When there's no solid basis, it's easy to divide people. "Partnership" makes groups dependent on the government. The funding comes with rules and outside control.

Government "help" has meant the end of political solidarity. Groups fight with each other and then go to the bureaucrats to look for answers. Psychiatry-oriented groups discredit real alternatives and people who are critical of the medical model.

O

ONTARIO PSYCHIATRIC SURVIVORS' ALLIANCE

O

The Ontario Psychiatric Survivors' Alliance (OPSA) was founded on January 27, 1990, by the Ontario participants of the Our Turn conference.

One of the people who helped start OPSA was Pat Black, then executive director of a mental health agency called Friends and Advocates Etobicoke (FAE), located in a suburb of Toronto. FAE was extraordinary because it was user-run. The board members were all ex-patients, and the membership determined everything that went on in the organization. It seems ironic, thinking about Pat, that we later warned people against ever involving mental health workers in their organizations, because they would take over and screw everything up. But very often that does happen.

Nevertheless, Pat and another FAE staff member who wasn't officially crazy—and a couple of other people who were the spouses of crazies—

founded OPSA, along with the rest of us, who were crazies. We had a very contentious debate at the first meeting that ended with the decision that only psychiatric survivors would be allowed to vote, although others who supported our principles could participate in meetings and influence discussion.

We discussed whether the term "psychiatric survivor" should apply only to those who had been locked up, or also to those who had been labelled and drugged but not incarcerated. Losing your freedom and being totally under the control of other people is a very different experience and puts you in a different position, politically, from voluntarily seeing someone to get help and being able to go home at night. But in the end, we decided you had to have received psychiatric treatment of some kind, but not necessarily to have been incarcerated.

Soon after that meeting, we connected with Pat Capponi. Pat is a crazy person who co-founded the Gerstein Centre, a nonmedical crisis intervention program in Toronto; the Supportive Housing Coalition, which develops housing for crazies; the Advisory Committee of Ontario's Psychiatric Patient Advocate Office; and the Ontario Advocacy Commission, an attempt to develop and deliver advocacy services to "vulnerable adults" (which has since been scotched by Ontario's Conservative government). She is the author of *Upstairs in the Crazy House* and *Dispatches from the Poverty Line*.

Pat had funding from the Community Mental Health Branch of the Ontario Ministry of Health to run the Leadership Training Program (later called the Leadership Facilitation Program). Her official mandate was to train people to sit on mental health-related boards and committees, in order to be part of "partnership." The idea was that any board or committee that dealt with mental health issues should include recipients of mental health services so that they could try to make the system more responsive to their needs. (The smartest thing I've ever heard about partnership, which I've often quoted though I have no idea where it comes from, is "How can we be partners when you're in a white coat and I'm in pyjamas?")

Pat would get together with crazies to talk to them about functioning on boards and committees and teach them about rules of order. But leadership facilitation was a lot more than that. It was about power and choice. Pat encouraged people to talk about their own experiences, which inevitably led into political discussion. Over the years, she has inspired countless people who didn't have any hope until they met her.

Pat Capponi

After I got out of the hospital in the 1970s, I lived in a psychiatric boarding home in Parkdale. I edited *The Cuckoo's Nest*, which we did from the house. It was just people in the boarding home, trying to say what it was like there. It was a very dinky, tiny little paper.

That's the first time I came up against something that's been consistent ever since. This little parade of professionals came up to me and said, "You can't call it *The Cuckoo's Nest*. That's very offensive." And I said, "Excuse me, I'm a crazy, and I'm not offended." That same kind of dialogue has been going on ever since. [Pat has always insisted on using the word "crazies," and gets a lot of flak for it.]

Anyway, after I got together with David Reville, we went to the papers with a story about our working group on boarding homes. The *Globe and Mail* picked it up. It was called "Nowhere to Go."

David and I organized a lunch in a committee room at City Hall that was to approximate a lunch in a boarding house. We invited the mayor and critics of the Ministry of Community and Social Services from the legislature to have lunch with a bunch of crazies. We served baloney sandwiches, and little packs of Smarties that were supposed to be people's medications. The "pharmacist" went around from person to person filling everyone's little cup. We passed them all around because of course that's the way it happened in the boarding house: you'd end up getting somebody else's dope. We had a bag of cockroaches. And we decorated the committee room with cobwebs. It was political theatre. We were trying to highlight the conditions in boarding homes.

The mayor came. He toyed with his baloney sandwich. He sort of opened it up, and said, "Oh, shit." To be as realistic as possible, we'd left the sandwiches out overnight, and they were really dried out.

In the early 1980s, I developed this proposal for leadership facilitation, just for the Parkdale area, called "Looks Like Up." I'd gotten into a fight about a personnel thing. I sided with a staff person who the Ministry of Health was trying to fuck over, for being a maverick. They said they'd only fund it if I shut up about this other thing. As soon as they told me the choice, I was on the phone to the assistant deputy minister in charge of mental health, telling him I was going to organize a demonstration.

This staff person had taken substantial risks, including giving me the "daily movement sheets," which showed who'd been killed—who'd died, I mean. And I would print those. So they really wanted to get her. It seems to me, if you let somebody hang out to dry who's helped the movement, nobody's going to be brave enough to do that anymore.

Some years later, I was sitting on the board of the Gerstein Centre. I was on five or six different committees, and it was killing me. Especially the hiring committee. Just the impact of the stupidity of the interviews. You had to choose from the existing stock of service providers. So I got mad. And they said, "Go get some other people, then." And I said, "How can I go get anybody when I'm sitting in these committee meetings all day?" I was given an office at Gerstein, and I started the first leadership group.

I'd found a lot of people during the hearings on community mental health legislation [the "leash-law" hearings], where they'd come out and told their stories, often for the first time. It was just a matter of playing "connect the dots." Here were all these people thinking they were all by themselves, and I got them together. We had the opportunity to connect, put stuff on paper, get stuff on video. Suddenly people were seeing each other in a different light, in terms of "What can we do?" rather than, "We're persecuted." It was very cool.

Initially, the point was to prepare people to sit on boards and committees so that they could influence mental health policy. But it quickly got into how to survive the manipulation. And then we figured out that we had to get the service providers' heads straight, or they'd massacre us. They were killing us with their games, so we had to make them realize the games they were playing. That process constantly evolved. The experience of the people participating changed from month to month; the problems, the scope. It went from "How do I make a motion," at the beginning to very sophisticated strategy stuff at the end—"How do we talk to these people and make them actually listen?"

I had lunch recently with a guy from Hong Fook Mental Health Services, which is for Asian crazies—mostly Vietnamese, Cambodian and Chinese. David Reville had got me on the board of the Clarke Institute of Psychiatry, and I got this guy on, and then I left. I didn't expect to abandon him on that board, and I still feel bad about that. He needs another crazy on there. But he's wonderful.

I worked with the Hong Fook group. I was worried about whether it was culturally appropriate for me to be doing that. I told them I didn't think it was going to work, but they all voted and decided they wanted me to do it. Their cultures are very big on respect for authority; respect for the doctor. And there's a deep, deep shame. They have a lot more to overcome, in a way. But it's wonderful—the crazies have already separated from Hong Fook. They've got their own organization now.

Watching this guy negotiate those mine fields on the Clarke board, and having seen fifteen crazies from around the province write provincial mental health policy—those kinds of things make me feel like the leadership program really succeeded.

I've learned so much about the inherent worth of people. And that's both elevating and a killer. It was so hard, in every group I ever worked with, even though nobody ever whined or said "Poor me"—but just hearing those stories! You feel this great pride, but it's balanced with all that pain.

I'd like to see our movement develop strong regional connections before we get to the wider ones, because it's too easy to become distanced from what's on the ground. I also want to see stronger cross-disability connections. The similarities between us and people labelled physically disabled blow me away. Somebody sitting in a wheelchair who's trying to take control would run into the same games, the same words. So you really shake people out of the idea that "This happens to me because I'm schizophrenic." It happens to anybody who's different. To strengthen those bonds would strengthen all of us. We're in the middle of a right-wing wave now, and we need to broaden the movement if we're going to keep fighting.

Above all, I want individual people to recognize enough about their self-worth that all else follows, so that any act of impinging upon someone's autonomy is met with legal and intellectual force.

OPSA's early days

Pat offered to do leadership facilitation with the non-Toronto people on the OPSA steering committee—her program's funding paid for them to travel in and stay at a hotel for the weekend. She'd have a leadership session with them, and then we'd have a two-day OPSA meeting. We'd have long Saturday meetings where people were already tired after the leadership facilitation program on Friday, and then a group of us would party on the Saturday night, which made the Sunday meetings even harder. It was not an ideal way to do things. It was exhausting. And the participants were in many cases people who had very quiet lives otherwise, and then all of a sudden there'd be these weekends from hell, with all this work and all these new ideas. But it allowed OPSA to be a genuinely provincial organization.

At the meetings, people from different places would talk about what was happening where they lived, and we'd try to decide what OPSA should do. I know that a lot of the people who attended, both from Toronto and from elsewhere, were really happy about these meetings and felt they accomplished a lot. But after a while, I didn't feel that way. I found the meetings tremendously frustrating. It was wonderful getting together and finding out what was happening elsewhere, but there was nothing happening at home.

In other parts of the province, people were starting groups, or transforming groups to which they already belonged. A CMHA group would say, "Okay, we're part of the CMHA, but we can also have our own group here that's part of OPSA." People were talking to each other about what had happened to them and feeling better about themselves, which was great. A lot of people were also joining boards and committees of mental health bodies; putting time and energy into these meetings where, I felt, they were tokens and nothing was going to change as a result. That, I found depressing; it seemed like a sad waste of time. I wanted the provincial office to be more active. I wanted to be producing a publication; I wanted to make the organization bigger and get more people involved. And I wanted OPSA to be funded.

In March 1990 there was an event in Ottawa called the Federal/Provincial Consultation on Mental Health, where the provincial government brought together nuts and bureaucrats to talk about mental health policy. This came about as a result of the "consumer participation" ideology. Each of us crazies had to sit in a small discussion group with some of the bureaucrats and talk to them about some aspect of policy. One of the people in my small group was John Trainor. Trainor, a mental health professional who had previously worked at the Queen Street Mental Health Centre, was to become the head of CSDI—the Consumer/Survivor Development Initiative. That was the funding body for crazies in Ontario. It was a project of the Community Mental Health Branch of the Ministry of Health; its mandate was to help develop consumer groups—which later came to be called consumer/survivor groups. (I've always found the term "consumer/survivor" even more obnoxious than the word "consumer" on its own.)

Trainor was taking notes at the end of our group session. My recommendation was that OPSA be funded. I was standing behind him, looking over his shoulder, and he wrote something like "consumer initiatives should be funded." And I said, "No. That's not what I said. I said OPSA. Please write down that OPSA should be funded." He did.

In April of 1990 we had a steering committee meeting where it was agreed that OPSA needed to have a coordinator. Randy Pritchard (who had spoken at the leash-law forum) nominated me for this position, and I was unanimously elected. This didn't surprise me, as I was friends with everybody, even though they weren't all friends with each other. I was hardline antipsychiatry (as was Randy by that time, having taken a closer look at the system and decided it was rotten to the core), but I didn't jump down the throats of people who saw things differently. I listened politely to different views, whatever I may have been thinking. I was gentle with people, whereas most of the other rigidly antipsychiatry people were more vocal about their rigidity, and less scared of people being mad at them. I think my terrible fear of people being angry with me enabled me to be extremely diplomatic. Some people saw my diplomacy as skill; I saw it as cowardice. But, whatever it was, it worked.

I put out the first issue of our newsletter, *OPSAnews*, in May of 1990. It was wonderful to be publishing again. I never felt at the time that I did my job adequately, in the sense of doing what I was supposed to be doing; that I really did, or could, coordinate anything. But I was really happy with the newsletter, which was a vital organizing tool. Chris Bearchell, my lover, did a great job designing it, which helped.

The first chunk of funding we got, besides a tiny amount of operating expenses, just provided me with a salary so that I could afford to work full time. After I started getting paid, I started working all the time. I felt more of an obligation, and I was getting paid handsomely. Someone had suggested that I ask for $40,000 per year, which seemed ridiculously high, but I got it. I felt guilty because I was getting paid and Randy wasn't, and he was working just as hard as I was. In fact, he was doing what I considered the boring tasks: office work, accounting, keeping things together. I was doing the "glory" work that I loved: travelling, media, public speaking, writing, publishing. I felt that he was getting shafted.

I think it was within a month of my being elected that he was sent away to Winnipeg. (Much earlier he had requested to be allowed to move to

Winnipeg and been refused.) Apparently his psychiatrist told him he was not to do any advocacy work; that he had to stay out of trouble and get a job, and bring his family there, and then they would set him free. I was sure they were lying. But he went.

I was terrified. I had agreed to be coordinator on the assumption that he was going to help me. I felt lost without him. I thought he was much smarter than I was. He certainly had a great deal more self-confidence, and I felt he had a much stronger grip on politics. I'd never concerned myself with current events, and he always had. He knew what was going on in the world. He read newspapers. He used to talk about "the big picture," and my sense was that he understood the big picture and I didn't.

Plus, I needed an ally: someone whom I was really close to, who was another crazy, and who was going to be in this with me through thick and thin. Suddenly I didn't have that anymore. Some people in the group asked what they could do to help me, but I felt like I couldn't even figure that out on my own. I had very little faith in myself. So there I was, feeling all alone and desperate. I was convinced that I was totally screwing up; that the organization was going to fall apart and lose its funding, and it was going to be my fault.

Eventually, I went weeping to Pat Black at FAE. I told her I felt I had agreed to do something of which I was completely incapable, and now I was going to let everybody down and make a fool of myself and waste this opportunity to do something good. I was a mess. I said, "I can't do this without Randy." She replied, "Of course you can. You have been. Several weeks have gone by since he left, and the organization is doing fine."

She pointed out that I'd assisted people in launching a new group in the Yukon without Randy's help. (They had been inspired in part by my radio show, "Analyzing Psychiatry," in which I talked about OPSA, and had subsequently invited me up there. I'd had a great time and done all kinds of media work and public speaking.) I'd also begun my Ontario travels in Randy's absence, flying to north-central Ontario, where I'd helped people start a couple of groups, and my work there was very much appreciated. Eventually Pat talked me into peeling myself up off the floor and going back to work.

But I still badly wanted Randy to come back. After a couple of months, he did. To my astonishment, his warrant had indeed been lifted, as promised.

His new freedom removed an immense psychological burden from him, and he was ready and eager to do more work for the movement. Meanwhile, OPSA had received more money, so I was able to get him hired as my assistant coordinator.

Other staff members came on at about the same time. One of our tasks was to get longer-term funding. A steering committee member was given a contract position to write the funding proposal for the year to come. Time passed, and it didn't get done. Finally, Randy and I sat down at a computer about two days before the proposal was due and wrote it. It was a masterpiece of deception. We said exactly what the funders (the Ministry of Health, which also funds the mental hospitals and all the community mental health agencies) wanted to hear: that OPSA was all about partnership and consumer participation. We never used the word "consumer," though; we used "psychiatric survivor." But we claimed that the idea of OPSA was to empower survivors to participate in making decisions about mental health policy; in the planning, implementation, delivery and evaluation of mental health services. This was not the least bit true, but it got the organization half a million dollars.

I believe that we did follow our stated mandate to the extent that our members wanted us to. But what was far more important to me was that we got a lot of powerless, beaten people thinking about their lives in new ways. Most of all, we got them talking to each other, and feeling stronger and less isolated.

It was a problem, though, that we had to portray OPSA as an organization that would be comfy for consumers as well as survivors; we had to make it seem that we were eager for more consumers to join. Randy and I, at least, didn't really feel that way. Much later, someone suggested to me that one of the reasons OPSA eventually fell apart was that it was founded on these kinds of lies. To some extent, this is probably true. But it was worth it. Many of the good things we did couldn't have happened without the money. And I certainly have no qualms about having taken mental health money. I believe they owe us, because they made a great deal of money in the course of taking away our freedom and destroying big parts of our lives.

Many OPSA groups found themselves with new troubles as soon as they received government funding:

"One thing that happens once there are paid staff people is that volunteer involvement and dedication drop off. The sense of community involvement slips away."

"They push us around, tell us what we should and shouldn't do. We're officially not allowed to do individual advocacy. That would be providing a service, and we can't do that. They're discouraging us from hiring a systemic advocate.

"When you accept government money you have to be answerable to different people. You have to jump through hoops, and write all these reports.

"Our consultant had a personal vendetta against our last coordinator. She'd get angry with him and take it out on us. She was phoning here twice a day."

"Directives should be on paper; never mind calling at ten to five and yelling and screaming for half an hour!"

"At first we said we were radical, that we'd fight this and fight that, sit on all these committees. Then we all burned out. We were fighting with each other. Then we got funded, and there was even more stress, with all the paperwork and criteria to meet. Now we're fighting with the funders. What I'm hearing more and more is, 'We don't care if the government pulls the funding. We did more when we didn't have any money.'"

The Randy and Irit roadshow

In May 1991, after a long time of me travelling and Randy holding down the fort back in the office, I decided I wanted him with me on the road to talk to OPSA groups. I felt I needed his stronger political style and problem-solving abilities. Besides, he knew how to drive, and I liked being with him.

But, from our very first time out, I stopped being the star. I was a pretty good performer, but he was superb. My style was gentle and soft, whereas he would go, "Okay, you've been treated like shit for years and years; maybe it's time to decide you're not going to take it anymore." A few people were scared by Randy's approach, but many loved it. I would get warm applause at the end of a talk, but he would get people standing up and shouting. That was when our funders got serious about pressuring us, saying that OPSA had an image problem; there was a perception that we were too radical.

I felt that Randy's approach and the response he got were great for OPSA. But it was not good for my self-esteem. I started feeling more than ever that he had it all, and I didn't have much of anything. That he made OPSA happen and if I dropped dead it wouldn't matter, but if he did it would be finished. I'd talk to him about that, and he would tell me it was nonsense; that none of this would be happening if I wasn't making it happen. But I didn't believe him.

In retrospect, I think that the softness of my delivery was essential. The combination of the two styles worked well. I also think OPSA might not have collapsed as quickly if it had been just me doing the public speaking. But it might not have been as effective, either.

New adventures, new staff

About the time Randy and I started travelling together, we heard that the crazies at the Peterborough CMHA "clubhouse" had rebelled. (Peterborough is a fair-sized city not far from Toronto.) Apparently, they were actually marching around outside the place with placards protesting the firing of their favourite staff person, Charles Henderson. We'd never heard of such a thing happening anywhere and promptly got ourselves invited there.

Charles said he hadn't been told why he had been fired, but as far as he could figure out it was for being friends with the members. He'd go out with them and he and they would visit each other's homes. He was seen to be fraternizing with them in a way that the CMHA found inappropriate.

It was Charles who had radicalized the people at the clubhouse. By their own accounts, he was largely responsible for most of them being on far lower doses of drugs than the people at any other clubhouse I had ever visited. He had encouraged everyone to take what they considered the smallest amount possible—which is what the doctors are officially supposed to do, but don't.

And the place was so different. Instead of staring at the floor and smoking cigarettes and maybe playing the odd game of cards, people were playing music and laughing and talking about things that mattered to them. They were awake and interested in life. It wasn't the usual artificial, grim atmosphere; it felt like somewhere people actually wanted to be. We were flabbergasted. And they were thrilled with us, and with OPSA, and formed an OPSA chapter on the spot. It was one of the longest-lasting chapters.

OPSA hired Charles as a "regional development officer" for that part of

Ontario (we were into using fancy terms to impress the funders). We were delighted with the idea of hiring someone the CMHA had fired. And he was, it turned out, one of us. He told us that night over dinner that he had been locked up, briefly, years earlier. He hadn't gone public before, because he had enough trouble from the CMHA without being tagged as a crazy.

He was sweet and caring and energetic. The clubhouse members were his personal friends. He had young children, and he'd have these people who were supposedly mentally ill come over and sleep at his house and play with his kids all the time. There was no notion of "us" and "them."

Around the same time, we hired another great person, Jennifer Chambers, as peer counselling facilitator (see page 123 for Jennifer's story). It was time to put our money where our mouth was in regard to alternatives to psychiatry. The principle of peer counselling is that you ditch the inequality inherent in a situation where one person is supposed to be okay and is getting paid and the other person is supposed to be sick and is getting help. Money is not exchanged. People are given some basic rules about listening and taught about the importance of expressing emotion, and then they exchange counselling sessions with each other. Curiously, the peer counselling position was the first to be cut by the government when arguments later arose about what jobs they were prepared to fund.

Shortly after Jennifer joined the staff, Kathy Horlock was hired to co-ordinate Rising Tide, OPSA's first provincial conference and annual general meeting.

Rising Tide

Rising Tide took place in September 1991, and it was stupendous. What pleased me most was that I contributed nothing. I was busy doing a television show for the series "Ideas on Camera" ("Toxic Psychiatry," in which CBC producer Max Allen talked with Peter Breggin and me about the dangers of psychiatric treatment) and didn't have to lift a finger to make the conference happen. I was very proud of OPSA's staff and volunteers.

Rising Tide was owned and operated entirely by nuts. Many OPSA members put on workshops. Most had never done anything of the kind before, yet they did it well. We had a great dance on the last night.

By that time, I'd made a few enemies in OPSA—mostly people who felt

Randy was a bad influence on me. But at this conference, all hostilities were suspended. We were all so happy and excited to be there. I partied with every one of the people I'd been having a hard time with.

Advocacy in action

By the time Rising Tide happened, Randy had become very good at helping people who were being shafted by the system. He was quick to respond and really interested in their situations and could often actually find solutions.

Once we got a call from another branch of Friends and Advocates, where the director was terminating the membership of anyone who complained about the organization. People were in a panic because they had nowhere else to go. This is where they would hang out all week; it was an important part of their lives. They didn't know what to do. Everybody seemed to be scared of this woman. So they phoned OPSA, and Randy said, "Okay, we'll come and fix it."

All I did at the meeting we attended was sit and take notes. Randy got people to tell him about what was happening. He said how outrageous it was that this woman was treating people this way. It ended with an official complaint to the Ministry of Health, which resulted in the woman being fired.

Another time we were told that people at a clubhouse up north would get demerit points for speaking French, because the staff didn't understand it. Apparently, if you got enough demerit points you had to do things like clean the toilets. We met with the nuts there first, and then with them and the staff. (This was our standard procedure when we talked with staff at all.) Randy encouraged people to present the issue directly to the staff in our presence; the talk we'd had before the staff joined us had given them the courage to do so. That was the end of the French problem. I know, because we actually had a follow-up meeting that time.

One of the things people were unhappy with, in general, was that we didn't do enough follow-up. It was true. We'd rush around getting people worked up and then we'd disappear and they'd be on their own. We were trying to do too much at once; there were too many groups and too much going on. As a result we'd come barrelling into town, give people a flash of hope, and then abandon them. We should have been training more people to work with the groups, but we never had time.

Up north

On our last big trip, in May 1992, Randy and I visited several groups in OPSA's north-central and northwest regions, and attended a big nut conference up in Minaki. The conference was co-hosted by the Fort Frances CMHA and the nut group there, the Sunset Country chapter of OPSA. Sunset Country was actually a network of small-town groups, coordinated by Susan Marshall (see page 148 for Susan's story), which had an extraordinarily positive, comfortable, mutually respectful relationship with the local CMHA. It was not your usual CMHA, and not the only relatively good one in that part of the world. "Up north" tended to be better than the rest of the province in many ways. There was more of a need to stick together because of the geographic isolation. And the mental health establishment was less powerful.

We did the tour, talking with people in several towns and then speaking at this conference. We talked, as we always did, about our own experiences and about OPSA. We said how inspiring the trip had been, and how proud we were of what people were doing up there, and how different it was from "down south." I think we made people feel really good. And by that time we had both developed some finesse: we were quite antipsychiatry, but in a way that was hard to argue with.

Then we got returned to Toronto. On May 21, Randy, Charles and I were called to a meeting with our funders. The director of Community Mental Health announced that Randy and I had screwed up on the trip. Apparently, we'd scared a couple of groups so badly that they'd decided not to be part of OPSA anymore. We demanded to know which groups she was talking about, but she said she couldn't tell us—it was confidential.

We were devastated. I wrote, "Time to resign" on my notepad. Randy told me later that that was exactly what had gone through his head at that moment. We both went pale and shut up after we'd tried and failed to get information about what had actually happened. Very soon after that meeting, Randy and I parted company with OPSA.

I guess I'll never know what really happened. The people we talked to afterwards, those we'd seen on that trip, said we'd been great. We had stopped in North Bay near the beginning of the trip, and the OPSA staff people there didn't like us. They were really conservative; the North Bay rep at one of the first OPSA steering committee meetings almost quit the group when we decided that OPSA would officially oppose electroshock. He later became a staff person. It may be that that group complained about us. But the North Bay chapter didn't stop being part of OPSA.

A short time later, OPSA was audited and Charles (who had since become coordinator) was fired by the board. OPSA was taken over by a couple of people who'd opposed me and Randy for a long time, including a board member who had once sent a letter to members saying that we were fascists trying to impose our own agenda on all the groups.

There was a weird meeting where Randy and I, along with a bunch of other people who'd been involved with OPSA, were called back to talk to the board about what had happened and what should happen. Randy and I both said, "If you want to save OPSA, move the central office up to north-western Ontario, where the strongest network of groups is." The Toronto location of the provincial office had always been a problem. People from every other part of Ontario resent Toronto. Also, it's where the provincial government is, which makes it too easy for them to interfere.

This advice was ignored. OPSA continued to function for a while after we left, and then stopped: the result of the audit and a government investigation initiated by a disgruntled former board member was a finding that the group was not using its resources to fulfill its mandate, and the funding was cut.

At first, Randy and I were going to start a national antipsychiatry organization, but it never happened. We started fighting with each other about politics. He felt I was out of line because I wanted to focus on creating alternatives to psychiatry. I think he felt that wasn't important compared to tearing the system down, which I don't think is possible. He thought I was being a wimp, and I thought he was being ridiculous. Randy and I parted on such bad terms that I was astonished when he agreed to be interviewed for this book.

Randy Pritchard

I think that, for a very brief period of time, the mental health system in Ontario was actually afraid of OPSA. This was marvellous. We achieved our true moment of power the day the CMHA walked into our office and wanted to negotiate a deal with us to fight together against the hospitals. Irit said, "Yeah, and we can arm wrestle afterwards to decide who gets how much funding." There was the head of Ontario Division, coming to us, wanting our backing against the hospitals. From that moment on, it went downhill.

What happened reminds me of the Who tune, "Don't Get Fooled Again": "Meet the new boss, same as the old boss." People come in trying to change things and you end up with a new set of bosses that take over, and it starts the cycle all over again. Someone decides, "Hey, I don't like what's happening here." It's inevitable in any type of movement.

I think anyone who wants to get into this line of work should go into it with a very specific timetable: "I will put my energy into this area for two years. And at the end of that, I'll voluntarily walk away." That would have been useful for all of us. There were a million different directions people could have gone in, and stayed in the movement. By constantly moving on, you guarantee that you don't try to control the outcome, and you guarantee new leadership because people will always step in to fill the vacuum. And those who would snipe at you no matter what you do—you give them less in the way of targets. So just get in, do what you're there to do, and get out.

There will always be people in this or any movement who are going to do the bulk of the work. And that's largely because of the failure of all of us to actually get serious about bringing leaders along. And I think part of that has to do with the attitude of "I want to become indispensable and therefore I will run myself into the ground." Leadership training should be focussed on people heading off to do specific tasks, and then there should be some kind of follow-up, where people come back together and talk it over. Bring people back in so they can say what they're encountering out there, and get some support.

There's a great truth about all movements, and it was certainly true of OPSA. You start off with a group of people who have similar visions. And in an attempt not to be exclusive, you invite everyone to join. Well, of course, you're going to end up diluting the original vision, if not totally getting rid of it. And that's exactly what happened.

OPSA started as an antipsychiatry organization. It was not that, a year before its death. You got the people who were involved in the beginning suddenly going, "What's going on around here? Where are we going? Who are these people who are our members?"

And OPSA developed too quickly. The closest we ever came to dealing with this was when we stopped Charles [at that time a regional development worker for OPSA] from supposedly developing more groups in his region. He was asked to start five and he was up to eighteen, and it wasn't sustainable. Why bother creating expectations if you haven't figured out how to sustain them?

Things would have gone very differently if we'd built up our structure to the point where the board, rather than us, had developed policy, and we had implemented it.

Still, the best times of my life were with OPSA. I met the most amazing people. I think of Chico in North Bay, and Bev Goodwin in Thunder Bay, and the group in Peterborough. How can you not love them? They're the greatest human beings I've ever encountered in my entire life.

And amazing things have happened in Peterborough since the demise of OPSA. Last spring, Bob Bowers [one of the leaders of OPSA Peterborough] kept that group together and harassed the shit out of CMHA, to the point where they divested themselves of the clubhouse operation and the staff position, and something like $13,000 in operating expenses. They gave it to the nuts! They said, "We've had enough." Negotiations went on for about four months, and it was so neat to sit in that room while the negotiating was taking place, and watch them concede defeat. When I last met with the group they were talking about establishing their own food co-op out of the house. I don't know if that happened. But here was a group that never had any money to begin with, yet stuck at it and stuck at it, and beat them.

○

It was I who felt beaten when I left OPSA and parted company with Randy. My whole life seemed to have fallen apart. I spent the next year or so lying around feeling sorry for myself. I thought I should be shot for the mess I'd made of everything. Then, in September 1993, I started getting over it—mostly by moving to Vancouver. But those two years of working with OPSA had been miraculous for me. And the organization did so much good. When I was interviewing former OPSA members for this book, many were justifiably proud of the wonderful things their groups had done, and were still doing.

People Advocating for Change through Empowerment (PACE) used to be OPSA Thunder Bay, located in northwestern Ontario. It was lovely visiting their office, which was actually a house. I felt like I was in someone's home. Half an hour after I got there, I was sitting at the kitchen table drinking coffee, laughing and trading stories with a bunch of people I'd never met before but who I felt I knew. One thing I noticed was that there were more Native Canadians in this group than in any other I visited.

Group members told me about some of PACE's accomplishments:

"One of the good things we've done is put together and distribute survival kits, with toothbrushes, toothpaste, soap, condoms, a notepad and pen, tampons and pads. We take them into the hospitals, to give to people who are being discharged. They also contain information about PACE, and a guide to local services. Some of the staff give us a hard time about handing out the kits. We ignore them, and go on our merry way. And doesn't that piss them off! One of them said 'You mean you actually want to give one to everyone on the ward?' and I said, 'Why? Do you think it would be better if we had a draw?' They asked a million questions, as if they didn't know what it was about. Finally, though, they let us in.

"At one point one of them said, 'We've got a problem with these little gifts you've been giving out.' I asked what it was, and they told us that someone had drunk the shampoo. I laughed and said that wasn't our problem; people can bring their own shampoo to the hospital anyway, and if they want to drink it, that's their business. I asked what they do if people bring shampoo and was told, 'If it's a glass bottle, we take it away.' So I pointed out that ours doesn't come in a glass bottle. She didn't know what to say. Then she let us distribute the kits."

"We do have an effect on what's going on in the community. There was a guy who did a 'What's your bitch' program on TV who was putting down psychiatric patients. He was making fun of them and implying that they were violent. We got rid of him."

"Every time one of us does public speaking or gets something published or any kind of publicity, seeds are sown."

"A lot of our members aren't going into hospital as often. There's no way of knowing how many committals haven't taken place because people had somewhere else to go. The more active we become in helping others, the less we use mental health services. People stop just sitting around thinking about their own problems. There are people who first came here unable to speak above a whisper, who are now enthusiastic volunteers."

Another former OPSA group, West End Psychiatric Survivors (in Toronto), was responsible for creating Psychiatric Survivor Pride Day:

"We had the first Psychiatric Survivor Pride Day in September 1993. It was a pretty amazing event. It was one of the biggest survivor street demonstrations I've ever seen. There were about a hundred and sixty people.

"And there have been other events, too. There was a festival of performances, poetry, art and music in April, at a local library. There were also information tables. Vern Harper, who is a Native elder, came and performed a healing ceremony to close the thing off. A hundred people came. It was advertised through postering, faxing survivors' groups, and by word of mouth."

West End Psychiatric Survivors avoided the pitfalls of government funding, by never asking for any. They raised all their own money:

"Once you start getting government money, you're vulnerable to it being taken away. For a grassroots operation, it's possible to raise one's own funds. To have garage sales and ask for donations of goods and services and operate on a small scale, without paid staff. Use people's photocopying services here and there. And get support from different sources, so that you're not beholden or tied to anyone. That's one route, and I think you can do a lot that way. You can publish flyers, you can poster. You can have public events. You can have marches."

West End Psychiatric Survivors was founded by Lilith Finkler. Lilith is a community worker at Parkdale Community Legal Services in Toronto. She has been involved in the movement since the 1970s and participated in many early organizing efforts, with a particular focus on antipsychiatry and feminism. Lilith currently advocates on behalf of and in conjunction with psychiatric survivors. She also teaches mental health legislation to law students.

○

Lilith Finkler

The survivor movement has given me strength. I spent so many years being ashamed. I'd think, "I'm a crazy person and I'd better be careful, because if I tell people I was locked up, they'll think I'm totally off the wall. They won't hire me or let me baby-sit their kids."

I'll never forget my very first full-time job. I was making furniture. I'd had this training—Introduction to Nontraditional Occupations for Women. And then the government had given money to employers to hire women for nontraditional jobs, and half your wages were paid by the training program. So I applied for this job, and I got it.

About a year after I started working there, my boss came up to me and said, "How come you never told me that you'd been on a psychiatric ward?" And I thought, "Where is this coming from?" A long time earlier, I'd spoken with an employment counsellor who'd asked me about certain gaps in my resume and what had happened to me in different periods. I told her I'd lived in a group home and explained to her about some of the emotional difficulties I'd had.

Well, that was promptly entered into my file on the computer. And the guy who gave the subsidy to my boss at work said, "We're not paying 50 percent of her wages; we're paying 75 percent." Because I was designated as mentally disabled! So my boss was told, "We're giving you this money because we don't think she's going to last more than a few weeks. But you took her—so have fun!" So who would hire me? He would have to be crazy to hire me. He had a loony-tune on his hands.

So then my boss says to me, "He told me you wouldn't last more than a few weeks, and now you're running the place." We had a pretty good relationship, so he was wondering how come I'd told him about other parts of my life but had never told him I'd been locked up. It wasn't an easy thing to talk about.

One of the things I got from the movement was the sense that I'm okay. And also that it's okay to have periods of time when you're living in a different world; that that's not necessarily a bad thing.

○

Many other people I talked to also found that their involvement with the mad movement and with OPSA in particular had made a big difference to them personally:

"OPSA changed my life. It gave me associations with people radical enough to help me realize that what I believed about the system might be true. It gave me a consensus, so that I didn't feel alone anymore."

"In the past the only place to go was hospital, then back home, then back to the hospital. Psychiatrists had complete control of our lives. Groups like OPSA are absolutely vital."

"OPSA is a place where you don't get jumped on for getting emotional or saying strange things. I'm not seen as odd here."

"Finally, here are people I can talk with about myself and feel comfortable, and not be judged. I've been able to make and sustain friendships with people like never before. It's meant more to me on a personal level than anything else. It's kept me alive."

"Before OPSA, there was nothing but things like Prozac Place [actually "Progress Place," a community mental health facility]. And if you wouldn't play their games, you were on the outside. They have a select group of people who will always be their members. Like most programs, they're not interested in getting people through, and out, and on their own. They have an interest in keeping their jobs.

"OPSA took me from the point where I was sure I would never work again and that I would kill myself sometime soon, to the point where, now, I'm working. And if I wasn't working tomorrow, I could find another job. It's not a problem anymore.

"Until I found OPSA, people were always telling me I was not worth much. They'd want to slap me into a program or something. I'd spent a number of years where all my outside contacts were social workers who saw me as product rather than as a person. And suddenly, I was being treated like a person."

"OPSA gave me a whole new life, and a whole new sense of myself—that I had something to say that had universal appeal, that everybody could relate to.

"I don't think I ever would have even considered getting off my medications if it hadn't been for OPSA. I got to find out about the struggles of other people attempting to do it. And there was all this information in the office about people successfully getting off. And I thought, 'Maybe, just maybe, sometime in the future, I might be able to do this too.'

"It was scary, but it helped a lot to have other people around who had actually done it. It makes it so much more real, seeing other people deal with it and get past it. I got so much support. There was never any pressure at all to get off the drugs. I appreciated that because, at the time, it was very tentative for me, just even considering it.

"Before I began to withdraw, I was on Carbamazapine [a neuroleptic], lithium [a "mood stabilizer"], Rivotril [a minor tranquillizer], Elavil [an antidepressant] and Levothyroxine [a synthetic hormone]. It turns out Carbamazapine and Rivotril aren't even supposed to be taken together or in combination with lithium. I'd been on all of them for years. My psychiatrist never told me. I came across this information in the *CPS* [a standard drug reference]. Until I started spending time in the office and talking with other survivors, it hadn't occurred to me before to look the drugs up. And what I saw in the *CPS* scared the shit out of me.

"There was never any pressure at all from OPSA members to get off the drugs. But now I'm off all of them, and I've started a life that I never dreamed I would have. It's like I wore an anchor on my back, and now I've thrown it away. When I was in the system, I didn't even know having a life was possible. I thought that was for other people.

"Now, I think, and I feel, and I see. It's a whole new existence."

MIGHTY MADWOMEN

O

Sue Goodwin, Jennifer Chambers, Gisela Sartori, Judi Johnny and Susan Marshall are five women I'm proud to know, who have a great deal to say about the mad movement and say it very well. I'll let them speak for themselves.

Sue Goodwin founded Psycho Femmes, a performance and music group for crazy women, in 1993. She is active with Cobblestone Theatre and Friendly Spike Theatre in Toronto; she loves the theatre because it sends messages to and from the heart. She has two beautiful sons who she hopes will grow up in a kinder world.

Sue Goodwin

I was in the Clarke Institute of Psychiatry, in Toronto, in 1991, with a diagnosis of major depression; I'd tried to kill myself some years earlier, when I was twenty-three. I was sitting there watching people get drugged, just as I was getting drugged, and nobody ever getting any better. And then they'd just push people out onto the street. And I thought, "Hey, wait a second. Nobody's dealing with the real reason we're all in here, which is that we've all had pretty bad lives."

I was feeling miserable. I felt that there was no hope. I'm a journalist, and I just sat there and observed. And I'd say to myself, "Holy shit, Goodwin, keep your mouth shut," because I realized I was somewhere where I couldn't talk my way out of things. I'd been used to covering some pretty grim stuff in really tight situations, and talking my way around things. But in the Clarke, they had total control of us all. Absolute control. If you blinked the wrong way, it was going to be harder for you. So I just played the nice person and was very quiet, and made sure I was out of the way when heavy stuff was coming down.

I was very distressed the whole time I was in there, thinking, "Isn't there anybody who's gone through the system and can see what it's like?" When I got out, somebody gave me a copy of *Phoenix Rising*. I read it, and I thought, "All right! There are strong people out there who've survived the system and written about it. Thank god." I was so happy when I read about that!

I felt a lot better whenever I got together with other people who'd been in the psychiatric system. I kept going to groups. And then I decided I wanted to start a women's theatre and music group.

I'd thought about how women have a lot of important things to say, but often when they get into groups with male psychiatric survivors, women don't feel free to speak. So I thought, "I'll start a group that's just for women." I'm not usually the kind of person who excludes anybody and I felt really guilty about it for a long time. But then I thought, "No. Otherwise women are not going to be heard." And I think women are a lot better at being crazy, and a lot better at having fun together and at expressing themselves together, than men are.

So I started looking for other women who identified as crazy, and wanted to be out there telling their stories. It's not easy, because they're pretty awful stories, our experiences as psychiatric survivors.

I'd started an art group about a year earlier. I was hoping that other crazy people would want to come and do art, and they did. So I thought, "Well, other crazy people are going to want to come and do theatre and music."

I was putting up notices everywhere there might be women survivors. It was hard getting a group of crazy women together. We've only been together for about a year. We've managed to play about twelve times.

We started out playing at a drop-in for psychiatric survivors. We played sing-along songs, but we also got in a few of our very political tunes about how the system makes money off us and drugs us to death. Those were scooted in, along with all the happy sing-along tunes.

Sandra is a very musical person. I'm not; I used to play French horn and guitar, but that was before I jumped in front of a subway and got a head injury and became unable to remember how to do anything. I can't read music anymore. But I can still sing. Sandra puts a lot of my words to music. And Natalie is schooled in clowning, so she's taught us a lot about the theatre part. I'd done theatre in high school. I'd always wanted to be a ham, but in my family I was taught to be upright and proper.

We do a theatre piece called "Ten Milligrams," about a woman in a psychiatric institution trying to keep her dose down. I think it's pretty grim, but other people find it funny. And that's good, because our idea was to present the message that the psychiatric system is not a healing place and is not beneficial for people. But we wanted to present it in a way that people would listen to. That wouldn't be heavy, or knock anyone, or call all shrinks jerks. We wanted to present it in a theatrical way, with lots of fun and music.

There's a very strong message, loud and clear, that the system doesn't heal you. But I think people listen to music and look at theatre a little more easily than they would pay attention to a person getting up and saying, "This is crummy, and this is why."

The problem is, we are all crazy women. There aren't really ego problems, because we don't have really great egos, but there's a lot of craziness involved. And right now everyone's quit. Again. It's happened before; about two months ago, everyone quit. Except me; I'm the one who started this thing, and I don't quit on myself. But I'm still going ahead and planning a fashion party and run-away show for February, which is a really down time for me. People who don't want to dress up in funky fashion stuff can dress up in their favourite outfit that they would run away from a psychiatric institution in. A couple of survivors have some great ideas about that. And we have another survivor, who's a really funny guy, who's going to MC it.

The other women in the group have called me and said, "I hear you're doing this fashion show." And I said, "Yup." And they said, "Well?" And I wondered, are they waiting for me to ask them to be involved? I asked Sandra, and she said she thought she would be involved. And I asked Natalie, and she thought she would too, but that there was no way she wanted to be involved in organizing it. And I'm just about to ask Joanne.

There are just the four of us involved. It was never big. I had visions of a troupe of twelve, but it didn't work out. A lot of survivors are not really people who go out there and lay their soul bare on stage.

One of us keeps suggesting that we should go after funding, but I feel that the second we got money, it would just rip us apart. I've been involved in psychiatric survivor organizations enough to know that. Once you get money, everyone goes for the cash and people don't worry as much about why they're there. Instead, they think about who's getting more money than the other person, and whether they deserve it. So I keep saying, "Don't worry about money; let's just keep playing."

"Supportive" housing

I'm co-chair of the Supportive Housing Coalition (SHC) Tenants' Association. We actually call ourselves Tenants for Tenants. I thought that was a really stupid name; everyone keeps asking if we're a tennis association. But it was chosen through a democratic process.

We're organizing against the SHC. They're well funded by the Ministry of Health and the Ministry of Housing. They're one of the few games in town that puts up housing specifically for psychiatric survivors. In order to get a unit, you have to be able to live on your own and take care of yourself, and usually you have a support agency in the community. I guess a majority of tenants see shrinks. But then there's a fair minority of people, like myself, who don't see shrinks at all but maybe see a counsellor or a therapist every once in a while. And there are people who have graduated out of the whole system, who've decided they're better off on their own.

The SHC puts up nice-looking buildings so funders and politicians and neighbourhoods think, "Wow, these buildings look so nice. Maybe the people will be just as nice." And the survivors in the buildings aren't seen as a menace to the neighbourhood. Very few people even know it's psychiatric housing.

But the buildings are substandard. They're not built very well. The SHC has just kept building, and getting bigger and bigger, and nobody ever takes a look at the buildings. The Tenants' Association recently got an architect who agreed to go take a look at this girl's unit. The building is seven years old. Her wall had caved in. And the architect said, "This has to be fixed before the winter." Otherwise, the same sort of thing could happen this year, only this time it could be the ceiling.

There are thirty-two SHC buildings around Toronto, and it wasn't until we started a tenants' group and started going around to the buildings to deliver flyers that we saw what bad shape they were in. They're all painted on the outside and have nice little flower beds, and you think, "Oh—these look nice." But inside— oh my god. The SHC has far fewer property administrators than they should, so when they take over a building, that building doesn't get enough attention.

Besides the buildings themselves, there's a communication problem. The SHC doesn't communicate with us tenants. We don't know what they're doing, so we don't know what we should be doing. And it makes us feel as if we're inmates again; the powers that be are taking care of us, and we can't do anything about it. The building managers only talk to us if we don't pay our rent. There's an SHC newsletter that's put out really sporadically. There hasn't been one for a long time.

They've hired five community development staff. I live in the biggest building, and there's supposed to be a community development person there fourteen hours a week. Well, we're lucky if we see the guy for two hours a week. And when he's there, he sits in the office and talks on the phone. He doesn't talk to the people in the building.

I sat on the board for about six months this year because I thought, "This is incredible. I have to try to get some information about what goes on here, and why they're doing such a poor job of delivering services to tenants." But in six months I was unable to get my point across. I was discouraged from bringing forward any tenant complaints or tenant issues or anything. They wouldn't answer my questions. They'd tell me this wasn't the forum for that sort of thing. And I'd be going, "Wait a minute; a tenant almost got killed in the building, and you don't want to hear about that at the board level? Maybe it should just go straight to the Ministry." And they'd tell me that was a conflict of interest!

One of the tenants in my building snapped, and tried to kill one of the women who lives there. And the SHC just wanted to keep it quiet. We'd all said things about this guy; we all knew he was going to blow and that he would hurt someone. That's what really got me angry and made me decide I was in it for the long term.

Every time I feel that it's a lost cause and that nothing is happening—that all the groups are fighting and everyone's losing their cash and everything is going tits-up, and I get really bummed out—there seems to be a group coalescing around some issue.

Everybody has different experiences, but we all share the common experience of being shafted by the system and made to feel as though we're less than other people. So I'm in it for the long haul. I'm not going to turn my back and say, "I'm okay now and I don't have to remember any of that." Anytime it looks like the government is trying to get us I'll get involved.

I think there's something special about being crazy. You have a lot more sensitivity and empathy if you're crazy, because you've had some hard things happen to you and you've been in situations that others haven't been in. You've been in hospitals where you've been treated like dirt and have had no rights. Or you've been somewhere else in the system where the same kinds of things have happened to you. Those experiences can create people who are more sensitive and caring.

I think it's good that there are people like us. And I think being crazy does help. When all else fails, you can howl at the moon, or just be totally nuts. I've gotten to the point where I think, "Okay, that's it, I'm going up to the roof and I'm going to jump off." And I go up to the roof, and I stand there and look out at Toronto. I talk to the air. I say, "I was going to jump off the roof, because this is absolutely it." And then I end up laughing at myself. And I'll go and call up one of my crazy friends and talk to them, and hear all about their antics. I like the crazy people I know a lot better than the noncrazy people I know.

Lately I've been thinking what it would be like if I woke up tomorrow in a world where most people thought that we weren't scary, that we weren't to be avoided. Where people cared about us and realized that we were just people who had been hurt.

○

Jennifer Chambers was one of the founders of the Ontario Psychiatric Survivors' Alliance and was briefly employed as OPSA's peer counselling facilitator. Her experience with community organizing began in 1983, when she started a group for bisexuals in Toronto. She was "the" bi speaker and interviewee until endless repetition made this a chore. She has developed many peer support groups. For the past four years, she has worked as facilitator of the Patient Council of the Queen Street Mental Health Centre (Toronto's provincial psychiatric hospital).

○

Jennifer Chambers

I see my role at the Patient Council primarily as that of an advocate. I try to restrain the use of restraints, affect legislation affecting psychiatric survivors, and inform people about psychiatric drugs and about their rights (writing and performing skits is the most enjoyable way to do this). I also do interviews and public speaking and have initiated legal action ranging from Review Board hearings to a Charter challenge. I generally try to put the people for whom the Queen Street Mental Health Centre exists in the position of being able to control their environment, starting with their own bodies and working outwards into the world.

The Council is a grassroots organization with a board elected by people who variously identify themselves as consumers, psychiatric survivors or patients. Most of the members have done time inside Queen Street (I did mine in a general hospital). Whatever power I have comes from having these people behind me. I act on their direction—so even if I'm out in front, I'm following. Part of my job is to take initiative in advancing the Council's goals. Always consulting with Council members slows my work down, but that's what makes us different from advocacy groups that are not controlled by the people they serve. If advocacy is about vulnerable people taking power, it should start with putting them in charge of their own advocates.

Some Council members believe in mental illness and the medical model; some believe that drugs and institutions do more harm than good. Some believe both. What we all share are the basic values of power for our people and protecting them from harm. The Council as a whole is opposed to ECT, forced treatment and other psychiatric assaults. All of us are opposed to overdrugging.

The Council is composed of board members and general members. General members can attend and vote at board meetings. Whenever people have attacked the Council for not representing all points of view, we draw their attention to our democratic process. The chair has to struggle to accommodate everyone and also

try to accomplish anything. Another difficulty is that many people don't like coming to meetings.

Power relations

My experience has been that when strong activists' voices come into play in situations like ours on the Council, the powers that be often respond in a way guaran-
teed to cause divisions. They'll choose the members of the oppressed group who
are most agreeable to them to work with. Money and positions will tend to flow
to, and stay with, those who will best fit into the existing system. The powerful
will choose the ones they deem reasonable (whoever asks for the least). And the
ones who come to have privilege feel gratitude not to the fighters, without whom
the powerful would never have given them a second glance, but to the powerful
who have bestowed favours upon them. In fact, the powerless will often join the
vested interests in disparaging the "radicals." We saw it in the women's movement. Female politicians who wouldn't have had the *vote* if it weren't for feminists
would state that they got where they did with no help from the women's movement. I try to be understanding, but how I despise such ungrateful back-climbers!

Recently the Council had to deal with a question of conflict of interest. The
Council supports the employment of people who have received psychiatric treatment. But if such people are hired by the hospital (which is done, incidentally,
without an open hiring process) and are now taking direction from and being paid
by hospital management, can they serve on a board whose sole function is to
advocate for patients at the hospital? Can anyone be expected to confront and
openly criticize their employer? The Council offered the compromise of becoming
the employer in such cases, but this was not accepted. The conclusion we've
come to is that this is indeed an instance of conflict of interest, and that no hospital employee should be a Patient Council board member.

The psychiatrist-in-chief is our official "liaison" with the hospital. When a
committee to look into abuse of patients at Queen Street was struck, he actually
suggested that he be the one to choose who would represent the Council on the
committee (of which he was not in charge). He wanted to be sure he would be
dealing with "reasonable" consumers! This reminded me of how profoundly grateful I am to all the "unreasonable" people who first turned a trickle of politicized
psychiatric survivors into a torrent.

Much of what the Patient Council tries to do at the Queen Street Mental

Health Centre is stonewalled. Queen Street is quite supportive of our social events and forums; it's the serious problems that we can't get addressed. And we have no decision-making power within the hospital.

Outside of Queen Street, legislators have expressed their appreciation of the Council. Organizations ask Council members to speak. My excellent co-worker, Erick Fabris, produces our newsletter, *Psycho Magazine*, which has featured such themes as whether mental illness exists.

We have done reasonably well for individual psychiatric survivors both inside and outside Queen Street. We've gotten people out—one after thirty years inside —found housing for homeless psychiatric survivors and helped people withdraw from psychiatric drugs. One day I went to visit an elderly woman on the psychogeriatric ward and found her restrained in a chair. The staff told me she'd been yelling and throwing things around. When I spoke to her she told me, crying, that she'd been in restraints in the chair for four hours and had wet herself while trapped there. I persuaded the staff to untie her, saying I'd stay with her for a while. She changed her clothes and we hung out together. There was no trouble at all. I don't understand how anyone could treat a person this way. What kind of help is this?

Several people at Queen Street have told me they were asked to inform staff if they felt suicidal. When they did, they were put in seclusion! I don't believe the staff at Queen Street are "bad"; I don't believe that there is such a thing as a bad person. But institutions are bureaucratic and dehumanizing, and the whole mental health system is oppressive. Those who work in it get caught up in hurtful ways of dealing with people.

The Council has received some statistical information on deaths, use of restraints, etc., in the hospital. But we had to wait a long time to get it, even though, as hospital staff readily admit, this is public information and should be readily available.

Two years after submitting the Council's demands regarding systemic issues, we have finally received a written reply. Our demands can be summed up as follows: an end to rights violations and abuse; Council access to information about alleged abuse; Council investigations of abuse; and a change in the power relations between survivors and staff. The response can be summed up as: No.

We have been officially allowed to put out pamphlets and post signs, but we have been waiting for a year and a half for Maintenance to get around to putting up our signs and pamphlet holders. We have been told that staff feel "assaulted" by the information in our pamphlet on psychiatric drugs, which is simply a copy of the information on side effects listed in the standard drug reference text!

We need more money than we get. There is only one full-time-equivalent staff position, and that is pitifully insufficient for the work we have to do. We're trying to represent the views of psychiatric survivors in the biggest psychiatric hospital in Ontario—Queen Street has about five hundred beds, and eighteen hundred out-patients. It is located in Parkdale, which is the largest psychiatric ghetto in North America. On average, it costs $10,000 per month to keep someone in Queen Street. Think of the housing and support an individual could get for half of that!

With more money, we might be able to get information that could help us save lives. We have an inquest report that says a woman died after having been in restraints at the hospital. In violation of the hospital's protocols, staff failed to take her vital signs, never released any of her limbs and gave her only about one cup of liquid in twenty-four hours. Her death was ruled as being from "natural causes." We'd like to reopen the case, but we can't afford to pay for the detailed records of the inquest or to pay a lawyer or a doctor to reexamine the case.

Charter challenge

The Council's greatest success so far has been a change we were able to make in the criminal code as a result of a court case we won under Section 15 (the equality section) of the Canadian Charter of Rights and Freedoms. It was the first time Charter protection from discrimination based on "mental disability" had been used in court. And, as far as I know, the Patient Council is the first psychiatric survivors' group ever to have been granted full intervenor status in a court case (meaning that we could present evidence, cross-examine witnesses and make arguments).

The defendant would have served about two years if he'd been found guilty of the crime for which he was tried in 1977. But instead, he was found "not guilty by reason of insanity" (NGRI)—and he's still locked up. Over the years, he has been put in seclusion for *months* at a time.

Until now, anyone who has committed *any* crime, no matter how minor, and who has been found to have done so because of a "mental disorder" [this is the terminology that has replaced the now obsolete NGRI] could be held in psychiatric custody indefinitely.

The review board decides whether people will be released based on the assessments of psychiatrists who never have to prove that a forensic "patient" is dangerous; rather, in order to be released, the "patient" has to prove that he or she isn't dangerous. And how can anyone ever prove that they will *never* be dangerous?

People convicted of crimes are given a sentence. They do their time and then they're out—and they know before they go in how long their sentence is. The only indefinite sentences for "sane" people are for those considered by the court to be "dangerous offenders" (DOs). In DO hearings, the court must present evidence of dangerousness based on past actions. But people judged to have committed a crime because of a "mental disorder" can be locked up indefinitely because of some psychiatrist's opinion that they *might* someday be dangerous. This is true even for people who have never committed a violent crime.

In recent years more and more Canadians have fallen for the right-wing solution for dealing with people who have been "unruly": lock them up and keep them locked up. People who hold this perspective have opposed our attempt to change the law on the grounds that dangerous lunatics will now be loose on the streets. This ignores the fact that there is already a law in place—Ontario's Mental Health Act—that allows people to be locked up in psychiatric institutions if they're considered crazy and dangerous. The procedural safeguards in the Act are fairer than those in the laws governing people in the forensic system. Our victory means that the "burden of proof" of dangerousness in such cases will be on the state, as it is for every other Canadian.

Dangerousness

There needs to be a clear method for deciding whether someone is dangerous. Previously such decisions, on the basis of which it is determined whether a person will be incarcerated or set free, have been based on the mere *opinions* of the people on the Criminal Code Review Board. As a result of our arguments, the judge found that section 672.54 of the Criminal Code "fails to require proof to a clear standard of probability that the NCR [not criminally responsible] acquittee is an unacceptable danger or risk to public safety. It fails to provide proper safeguards to ensure that only those NCR acquittees who are shown to be risks to cause harm unacceptable to society will be detained under the Criminal Code." So the judge struck down that part of the Criminal Code!

Unfortunately, the Crown has appealed the decision. But the good news is that we have once again been granted intervenor status by the court. I just hope we can get legal aid.

The business of "proving" dangerousness is going to be very interesting. For several years, I taught university tutorials about analyzing scientific research. For this court case, I did some analysis of the relevant scientific research. There is *no* method of accurately predicting dangerousness. When I analyzed the statistics on the "best" rating scale they have in Canada right now, I found that the accuracy rate of the scale for predicting a person's future dangerousness was, on average, 19 percent. In other words, they'd be wrong about 81 percent of the time! Flipping a coin makes for much better odds. But the assessors are really excited about this great new scale and are using it.

The reality is that psychiatry has no expertise whatsoever in this area. One extensive study of forensic assessments (by Simon Fraser University criminology professor Robert Menzies) found that "clinical judgements" are, to a great extent, just police accounts rewritten in psychiatric jargon. Furthermore, the study found that the people judged to be dangerous were actually *less* so than the people they said were not dangerous!

Psychiatric survivors and the police

The assumption that people who are labelled "mentally ill" are dangerous (combined with similar racial stereotypes) may have contributed to the shootings of some Toronto citizens by the police.

For example, when Lester Donaldson, a black man labelled schizophrenic, was yelling in his own apartment, neighbours called the police. (Donaldson was lame from a previous incident of being shot by the police.) My understanding is that his wife offered to try and calm him before the police came in, but they went ahead. He was in a darkened room, playing music and eating his dinner. The police came in, turned on the light and yelled at him. He got excited back, and started waving around the paring knife that was in his hand. They shot him dead.

Police have the same prejudices against psychiatric survivors that the rest of society does. The difference is that they are called in to deal with situations involving survivors—and they're armed.

The best possible outcome of any potentially violent situation can happen only if you have some idea of the feelings and needs of the person involved. To find this out, police (and others) must go to the source. I asked people who have received treatment at Queen Street and been subdued for being violent what could have prevented or defused the situation:

"All I really wanted was space. I thought I was defending myself. I felt so crowded, overwhelmed. If anyone came near me, I let them have it. If they would have just kept their distance, I would have been okay."

"I wasn't being violent. I broke a window accidentally by slamming a door against it when I opened it too hard. Then when people started yelling at me and tried to contain me, I panicked and started fighting."

A few years ago I was part of a group of people that made a presentation to the Police Services Board about the possibility of psychiatric survivors formally sensitizing and educating the police in the course of police training. The Solicitor General's Office (SGO—the body in charge of the police) was considering funding our proposed program. We met with the police chief. A pilot project was going to be focussed on Parkdale. Unfortunately, a police job action resulted in the SGO's funds being greatly depleted. A new SG was appointed. The next thing we heard, the training of police in regard to dealing with psychiatric survivors was being handled by mental health professionals at the Clarke Institute. But mental health professionals are no better at handling escalating situations than the police; they're just armed with different stuff. Some are good, some are not—it's a matter of common sense, compassion and understanding, not professional skill. We want to open the door for police to hear from the real experts: the people who've been there themselves.

○

The Second Opinion Society (SOS), located in Whitehorse, Yukon, is the only antipsychiatry group I've ever heard of that receives government funding. Among many other impressive accomplishments, SOS has published an excellent booklet in plain English on psychiatric drugs.

SOS member Dorothy LeBel initiated a successful legal action against the people who had incarcerated and drugged her in 1987. The outcome was that a nurse was found liable for having falsely imprisoned her. In May of 1994, the Yukon Supreme Court found the nurse to have breached Section 7 of the Charter of Rights and Freedoms, which states that "Everyone has the right to life, liberty and security of the person and the right not to be deprived thereof except in accordance with the principles of fundamental justice."

Dorothy's is a landmark case in the history of the Canadian mad movement.

Gisela Sartori, one of SOS's founders, has been involved in antipsychiatry work since 1981. A psychiatric survivor herself, she is presently coordinator of SOS. She is also the author of *Toward Empathy*, a manual for training women's shelter staff to work with psychiatrized women.

O

Gisela Sartori

I was very involved in the antipsychiatry movement in Germany in the early 1980s. Then I came to Canada in 1985, and fell into this big, big hole, because there were a lot of people around me, especially in the social service field, doing things that really appalled me. And I felt very alone. In the beginning, I coped with it by saying, "Oh, this is all horrible. In Berlin, everything is different." I focussed on how dreadful it was that in the midst of this beautiful landscape, people seemed to be living in another age.

I lived in Vancouver from 1985 to 1986, and I went to the Mental Patients Association at that time and found it really frustrating [MPA had abandoned its radical roots by then]. In 1986 I moved to Whitehorse and got together with [antipsychiatry activist] Stewart Jamieson. That was the beginning of me getting myself established again. When we started SOS, I felt a sense of continuation from my life before. It wasn't enough just to connect with people here. Reaching out to other groups was the most important thing for me: being able to see SOS as part of something bigger.

From the very beginning, we've had special events and guest speakers—bringing people in from the outside—and it was always great. We're a very small group, and we started with no experience in doing things like this. But our enthusiasm carried us through. There was not one event that wasn't well planned and organized. SOS has a very good reputation in town and with the government. It's known that whatever we do, we do it right. The expectation was that we would screw up; that a group run by people who were supposedly mentally ill wouldn't be able to get it together. But we've always had good publicity for our events and lots of people showing up. We've reached different kinds of people, including, sometimes, people we didn't expect to reach.

We've chosen really interesting speakers; having them come up always gives us such a boost. And again, having people come up who are doing the same kind of work we are, but in other places, brings us a bit of perspective. It puts it all in a bigger context, which is really important not just for the "in group" but also for the people who are interested in what SOS is doing. They need to realize that it's not just this tiny little group in Whitehorse; that there is something more happening out there.

SOS has done a lot. I think it's impressive that we've been able to exist and to keep getting funding for all these years. Furthermore, we've managed to frighten the medical and social services establishment here in Whitehorse. We've also been given unbelievable local press coverage. Whatever we send in gets published, and we've educated the press not to use stigmatizing language about psychiatric survivors.

The main motive for starting this group wasn't to support or help each other. We wanted to get a second opinion out. That's where our name came from. Stewart and I were so frustrated by the articles we were reading that came up from the press down south. They always presented the medical point of view. So it was really important to us to talk about things from our point of view. Thanks to SOS, people who get abused by the system have somewhere to go to get information that is normally kept from them.

What has happened in regard to providing personal support has been really interesting. When we started, I thought we'd be swamped by people in extreme crisis. I thought the phone would be ringing twenty-four hours a day, with really desperate people reaching out to us. That hasn't happened. In some ways, I'm really happy that it hasn't.

I think one factor is that many people who have a long history of psychiatrization are so much in the clutches of the system that they never get free enough even to phone a group like SOS. And then, people perceive us more as an advocacy group than as a support group.

We have had people come in really desperate, and we've talked with them for hours. But it's not ongoing support. Sometimes when people come because their life is a mess, it seems that just coming in and spending time here is enough. This is so different from what I thought would happen.

Often people's friends or relatives call and want them to come for support. It's really hard for family members to understand when we say that people have to come of their own free will; that they can't be pushed into coming. When people make appointments and don't come, we never call them up and bug them. They have to be at the point where they actually want to come on their own. But that can be really difficult. People are so used to being pressured to get help. When they come to us and we tell them, "You're very welcome to come here, and you're welcome to phone when things are tough, but the initiative has to come from you," they sometimes find that a big barrier.

I think that *Second Opinion*, our newsletter, is in some ways the best thing we've done. The two issues we've put out so far have been beautifully designed and full of powerful articles. One of the shortcomings of SOS has been that we haven't reached enough people. I think the newsletter has really helped turn that around. It's brought many people into SOS.

Needs assessment

Soon after SOS started, we received funding to do a needs assessment: a survey of what psychiatric survivors need most. We had been invited to a meeting together with the Canadian Mental Health Association (CMHA) at the offices of the Ministry of Health. The CMHA had six or seven bureaucrats and a staff person who worked for the Challenge Program—a vocational rehabilitation program. Stewart was on their board of directors. Before the meeting, they said we should support their proposal for a halfway house, which we'd never even read. They handed it to me on our way into the meeting.

Joyce Hayden, who was Minister of Health at the time, put their proposal on the table and said to them, "Where are the *people* in here?" The ideas in their proposal were very medically oriented and controlling. It was unbelievably bad, and she didn't want to fund it. That was when she asked SOS to do the needs assessment. This made the CMHA furious. But we felt it would be outrageous for their proposal to be funded, and Joyce and her deputy minister Gay Hansen absolutely agreed with that.

Then the CMHA got lots of politicians involved. Finally, Tony Pennikett, the leader of the NDP government, came to Joyce Hayden and told her to fund their proposal, despite the fact that she didn't believe in it. So they started up the housing project, and it blew up in their faces. It was a horrible mess. When everything went wrong with that project, we were asked by the government to help save it. We didn't want to, but we tried. But it was too late.

At the same time, we were doing the needs assessment. The amount of work involved was enormous. For a long time, I felt that it was a mistake to have taken on this project. We'd never done anything like it, so it was this big, big thing that hung over our heads and took our energy away from our other work. I almost wanted to give up. But the wonderful Statistics Department people who were helping us kept telling us this would be important. And, looking back now, they were absolutely right. It took twice as long as we thought it would, but it gave our group a really good foundation. We had the voices of Yukoners and we could say, "Here, this is what people want." It gave us a lot of credibility.

The vehemence of the establishment's reaction amazed me, because I always think of SOS as a piddly little group. The moment it was discovered that we'd received funding to do a needs assessment, there was a huge outcry on the part of people in social services and in the medical profession. For example, the medical council wrote letters to the editor saying things like, "How dare they let this group interview other people who have experienced the psychiatric system? They'll all jump out the window!"

Mental Health Services refused to participate in the needs assessment, saying that they didn't want to subject their clients to what was sure to be an inferior study. They said to us, "We are the psychologists. We are the ones who should be doing this, not you."

Meanwhile, the federal Health Promotion people are calling it one of the best participatory research projects that has ever been done in Canada. I strongly recommend that other groups take on similar projects; when you have the numbers behind you, it's much, much harder for the government not to fund you and not to support what you're doing. Conducting a needs assessment doesn't have to cost a lot of money. And this is a good example of how important it is for groups to connect with each other; the work doesn't have to be redone by every group.

Resistance to SOS

Local professionals have never stopped trying to discredit us in every possible way. For example, when we tried to send a survey to doctors, it all went straight into the garbage. That's the medical profession; we expected it from them. But I think that the resistance from Social Services and other organizations—the transition home, the Family Violence Prevention Unit—is even more serious. People who are clients of these services are constantly being told that what we do is dangerous, that it will be bad for them—that they should stay away from us at all costs.

The reaction of Mental Health Services to our first newsletter—which we thought was very mild—was tremendous. They called up saying they were appalled by the inflammatory, negative newsletter we'd sent out and by how much harm it would do people.

I think it's very significant that "mental health" workers, who are supposedly in the business of helping people, put so much effort into keeping people away from others who have been in the same situation. People are supposed to come to them individually and be told what to do: essentially, to take psychiatric drugs. They don't want people to be informed. They don't want people to come together and devise their own strategies. It's really about keeping people isolated, seeing them one by one, and treating whatever they say as if it's all in their heads and has nothing to do with their social situation.

Professionals work really hard to keep people from realizing that how they feel has a lot to do with their lives and with society in general. I think they're unwilling to inform themselves. They have learned this very narrow, medical view in school and they never question it at all. I think it's a question of power: here in Whitehorse, they obviously see SOS as threatening their power.

Challenges

What I want SOS to achieve may be impossible. I'd like us to keep up our strong advocacy work, and to continue to be really outspoken about our antipsychiatry stance. And, at the same time, I'd like the group to be used by more people. To be available for people to use in the process of consciousness raising, and supporting each other, and changing things. Right now, SOS has a core group of people who work here or are on the board, and others who are using it as a service. I would like it to be owned by more people.

Unfortunately, it's a very long, slow process for people to change from clients into the owners of something. And then, there's a great deal of pressure from the government for us to water down our views. We argued a lot about whether to accept government funding. My position is that I wish we didn't need the funding, but I wouldn't be willing to do the work I'm doing now without getting paid. I'd come to meetings, but I wouldn't spend forty hours a week.

We've also had lengthy discussions about whether we should be strictly an advocacy and information group and not do any support. All of us are primarily interested in public awareness, advocacy and systemic change. And none of us really knows how to do support. But in Whitehorse, all there is for people in distress are oppressive social services and the hospital. And, looking at that situation, I think it's outrageous to just sit there and say how bad this is. People come and say, "But what can we do?" And we have to say, "We don't know. There isn't anything to do." I feel really strongly that our group has a responsibility, at the very least, to push for the development of something more helpful to people than what's currently available.

I think it was a very big mistake to involve only people who've been psychiatrized, as we did at first. I wish we had been quicker to include others who strongly agree with our political stance. We needn't let them vote on things, but we should work together with them on what we decide to do. For the first three and a half years, we didn't do that. Of course, it's hard to find such people in a small town. In fact, it's difficult for people even to come to SOS. The moment someone sees you walk in the door, you're stigmatized. We've started support groups, which people have said they want, and they don't show up. It can be really difficult to open up about yourself when you can't be anonymous.

Another problem is that we who work at SOS know all the professionals. We meet them at the grocery store. That's the most difficult thing for me: hearing, day in and day out, all these stories about how the system tries to keep people powerless, keep them away from ever dealing with the real issues in their lives, keep them away from each other—and knowing the people who are doing it. In Berlin, it was easy to be outspoken about the horrendous things these people do. Here, it's a lot more difficult to do this and name names, with everyone knowing everyone. What costs me the most energy is dealing with that anger every day, and trying to find a release for it.

The biggest obstacle to SOS's progress has been that, being in a small, isolated community, it's impossible to find ten strong antipsychiatry activists. We could have done a lot more than we have, but we haven't had enough people. There's so much work to be done.

Still, looking at the last four years, I'm astounded by how well we've worked together, despite our difficulties. I think this is primarily because none of us is interested in being part of a nice little "consumer" group, trying to make the mental health system work better. We are all clear that we want this to be a liberation group. That's the main reason we still exist—that we all have that point of view.

No advocacy!

The Conservative government here decided not to fund advocacy groups. When all these groups got letters saying their funding would be cut, we were sure we would get one too. But, thanks to Gay Hansen, who sold us as a nonadvocacy group, our funding wasn't touched. We are supposed to be a self-help and support group that does public awareness, but no advocacy.

So our proposal had to include a major focus on providing support. And we have done as much of that as we could, both in terms of individual support and by starting support groups and a peer counselling group. The point, though, is that they don't want us to challenge psychiatry; they want us to offer services. Not as a substitute for the mental health system, of course, but to "complement" it. Mind you, there isn't much of a system here. There's one psychiatrist and one mental health nurse in the hospital.

SOS and the community

The government has always pressured SOS to collaborate with social service agencies, which we don't want to do. But we do think it's important to connect with grassroots groups. For example, we've worked really hard on changing the views of some of the people at the Women's Centre. One of our members was badly screwed around by them. They didn't respect her confidentiality and she ended up being locked up. Since then, we've managed to force them to put a confidentiality policy in place. They've attended some of our events and we've seen a big difference in the way they operate. They've realized that psychiatry is a women's issue. Ads for SOS now appear in all their publications. They call and invite us to submit articles. When they first stopped being resistant to SOS, they referred a lot of people to us. Now, after having attended many of our workshops, they don't have to do that as much; they've figured out how to deal with situations that come up.

Many groups refer people to SOS; especially those that deal with really poor people, like the Salvation Army, Mary House (a Catholic drop-in) and the Native Friendship Centre. Even the psychiatric nurse at the hospital sends people to us! We also have good connections with the AIDS Alliance and the Health Action Network. We've put our issues on other groups' agendas, which I think is really good. We've had many excellent letters of support when we've applied for grants. I believe that if the government tried to get rid of SOS, a lot of groups would stand up for us.

Making links with other groups breaks through that whole problem of "us and them"; the idea that "mentally ill" people are from another planet, and that our issues have nothing to do with other people. I think we've changed that in Whitehorse, to some extent. A realization has begun to develop, that we're not so very different; that our issues overlap with those of other groups.

But we need to make far more effort to connect with people who have disabilities. Judi Johnny, who uses a wheelchair, has shown a great deal of interest in being part of SOS. For a while, we had board meetings at her house, but then we felt that was too much trouble and gave up on it. We made sure that some of our events were accessible and invited her to come to those. Last year we tried to make our old office accessible. But it was complicated, and we decided it wasn't that important. Judi was very upset. And people got annoyed with her. There was an attitude of, "What does it matter when it's only one person?" I always said I'd be furious if I was that one person and couldn't attend events. When Bonnie Burstow came to speak, one of the collective members booked a venue that wasn't accessible, and we had a big fight about it. I can't absolve myself of responsibility here; I didn't go out of my way to find a wheelchair accessible space. It was a side issue.

Now, Judi didn't just want to drop by every month. She wanted to be on the board. She wanted to be actively involved, and she had shown commitment to our issues. And somehow, we thought we had more important things to think about. She has tried very hard to get us to see ourselves as part of the disability movement. We came to the point of saying, "Yes. We're disabled; we don't have an inherent disability, but the system has made some of us disabled." But, during all our discussions of this issue, I've felt that there was a demeaning attitude toward people with disabilities.

After all, we get furious when the media call us "mentally ill" or "mental patients"; when they use words that are unacceptable to us. Language is really important to SOS. Yet none of us has ever made the effort to find out which words are acceptable in the disability movement. Language is changing there too; there are new words, and words you're not supposed to use anymore. And I get them all mixed up; I don't really know what's acceptable and what isn't. And I know that I haven't paid enough attention.

Another thing about SOS is that it's mostly white. There are only two Native people in the group, though others attend events. We've been told very clearly by the Council of Yukon Indians (CYI) not to interfere with Native people; that they do their own stuff. But they haven't done anything in the area of psychiatry. Native people who get locked up are subjected to the medical model, and CYI seems to have bought that.

Still, we take our newsletter to CYI. And now we've planned a series of community trips, during which I will meet with a lot of bands. Many of the small communities in the Yukon are 85 or 90 percent Native. We do have a strong connection with the Native Friendship Centre, and I went to the Native Healing Conference, which was wonderful. So there have been token attempts. But we have no Native staff members.

An advocacy story

A member brought a woman to one of the first SOS meetings who was desperately looking for people to help her get her child back. Before we met her, she lived in a cabin in the bush. She was very attached to her child and had very strong feelings about how to raise children. She didn't want to put him in day-care; she wanted to be with him all the time. She was very nonrestrictive.

It all went well until, at some point, she decided to try to get social assistance. The social workers thought her child was too spoiled and that she was too close to him and isolated him too much. She lived in a little place where there were mice. She thought that was neat; she and her son talked to the mice, who lived in the silverware drawer. But the social workers didn't see it the same way; they said her place was infested with rodents. They told her she couldn't live like that with her child; that it wasn't good for him. They said she had to live somewhere where she could find work and her son could go into day-care and have contact with other children. She fought that for a while, but then agreed to move into an apartment in Whitehorse.

This woman is someone who really needs to be out in the bush. She became more and more unhappy. She cried a lot. And of course, they used that against her, saying it wasn't good for the child. They ended up taking him away and putting him in a foster home. The woman was frantic. Twice she went and got him and took him home with her. That prompted them to lock her up and tentatively diagnose her as schizophrenic. They sent her down to the University of British Columbia Hospital in Vancouver for a four-week assessment. The psychiatrists concluded that she was not schizophrenic; she was just very upset about her child being taken away.

Then there was another incident where she took the child and threatened a social worker, so they put her in a forensic institution in Calgary. Four weeks later, she came back with another assessment saying that she was not crazy but was depressed about the loss of her child.

At this point, they took the child out of the Yukon and put him in a foster home elsewhere. She didn't know where he was. She had no access to him at all and was in tremendous pain. That was when we met her. The only thing she wanted was to get her child back. Her clothes were ripped and dirty; she was always pulling her hair out. She had no home. She lived on the street and got raped often.

We talked to her and offered to go with her to a lawyer. That was the best way we could think of to support her. We came up with these steps that she'd have to take in order to get the child back. The main point was that she needed a place to stay; no one would ever give a child back to a homeless mother. She moved in with an SOS member but ran away after a few days. We tried to find her an apartment, but she wanted a cabin. And no one wanted to rent to her, because she was in such a state and had no money. She was no longer willing to try to get social assistance after the terrible experience she'd had.

The group member who had been her friend and brought her to SOS in the first place organized a meeting of everyone who knew her and was willing to help out. There were about fifteen of us. But she wasn't prepared to do what we wanted her to do. It made perfect sense to us that we should ask her to get a place to stay; to do her laundry and change her appearance so that she wouldn't look so ratty and run-down. But she wasn't having any of it.

I'll never forget the moment when we drove down to the house of one of our members, and she sat in the car and howled like a wolf. Looking back, now, at that howl, I feel that I should have understood what it actually meant. I have a child, and I can imagine what I would feel like in this woman's situation. She ran out of the car, and I got very upset with her. We were all unbelievably frustrated. The opinion in the group was that she didn't want to be helped, that she played these games and didn't actually want to change anything. That was our judgement. And the support began to dwindle away.

As we withdrew more and more, she continued to hitchhike through town, telling everyone her horrible story. I often thought she'd end up dead in a ditch. Then her friend told us she was in a relationship with a man she'd met while hitchhiking. We were stunned that someone who was the way she was at that point could get into a relationship with anyone.

For a long time, she didn't come to SOS. But then she showed up with this man, who she's been with ever since. He's a wonderful, kind-hearted person. They got a lawyer and tried to get her child back. During that period, they came to SOS sporadically, asking for support. We told them what we thought; that they should take one of us with them when they went to Social Services or Children's

Services. That would happen, but then they wouldn't show up for weeks. Then they'd come again and ask for our help. We were always there to do what they asked us to do, but it was never consistent help; they had their own views of how things should be done.

Meanwhile, the woman had changed a lot. She was not as distressed anymore. She still desperately wanted her child, but her desperation was no longer so obvious to the outside world. There had been a court case, which they'd lost, and the child was put with a family that everyone thought would adopt him. Then they were informed that the adoption plan had fallen through (legally, the birth parent has to be informed when that happens). The child once again became a ward of the state, which meant that she could apply for access to him.

She found out that the adoption had been stopped because her son had developed Tourette Syndrome [which causes involuntary twitches, tics, shouting and swearing]. It turned out that he'd been diagnosed hyperactive and put on Ritalin, and then developed Tourette. So now he's on Haldol for the Tourette!

He is nine now, and has been gone for five years.

After the adoption fell through, the position of the social service people changed. They suddenly stopped saying there was no way she could get her son back. It turned out that a psychologist, an expert in child custody cases, had assessed the child and said it would be detrimental to him to be put into another foster home. And, thanks to the Tourette Syndrome, the likelihood of adoption had become extremely small. Children's Services never wanted to give the child back to her, but they didn't want him to be a permanent ward of the state, either. So they hired a psychologist and brought him up to do an assessment of this couple.

They found that she was in a stable relationship with a man who had it together. This, in combination with the Tourette, made them change their line. The psychologist did two days of testing and decreed that she should have access to the child but that it should be a very gradual process. The report was positive, except that he felt it didn't matter if it took two or three years to resolve this.

Throughout this process, which has taken a year, the woman and her partner have gained a lot of confidence; they no longer just accept whatever anybody says. So they felt encouraged to take the legal route again. They're appalled by the injustice of what happened to her and her son. With the help of another SOS member, they've gotten hold of all the files from Mental Health Services, Children's Services and the lawyers. And the things that were written about her were horrendous.

One of the main things Children's Services had always said was that this woman loved her child too much. That was very hard for her to understand, how anyone could love a child too much. Looking at the whole story and the people who have been involved, it was clear that none of it would have happened if she'd been in a relationship with a man to begin with. And then, lots of things were held against her not only because she was a single mother, but just because she was a woman. People would have thought it was fine for a man to live the way she was living, alone in the bush.

When the psychologist was here, he interviewed three of her witnesses, including me. I spoke to him for an hour. He also interviewed her doctor and someone from her partner's band [the partner is Native]. And absolutely nothing that any of the three of us said entered the report.

When he interviewed me, I was trying to make him understand this woman's situation after the child was taken away. He had accepted all the horrible views that people had of her; that she wasn't fit to be a mother, and so on. I talked about how wrecked she was when we met her.

But I've thought about this a lot, and it makes so much sense to me, that she lost it. And that's where I feel bad about how SOS dealt with the whole thing. We really wanted to help her get her child back, but we felt we knew how she had to make that happen. When she was unable or unwilling to do what we thought she should, we were angry with her. We set the timetable. We said, "Now it's time for you to get your shit together and do all these things, and that will show that you're really serious about this." When she didn't do what we wanted her to, we decided she wasn't serious. But in reality, she was in too much pain to be cooperative.

I think that if I had to do it again, I would just be there for her more, without pushing her to do things the way we wanted her to. If we'd let her have more time, the whole thing might have taken two years, instead of five. But we thought it should take three months. We didn't have years of agony in mind. We thought we'd fight this in a really disciplined way, and then it would all be over.

She always came to us and said, "They want me to wear high-heeled shoes and dresses." We never thought she should do that—but only because none of us do that. Whereas her social workers do. But we wanted her to be neat and clean and stop pulling her hair out and stop looking ratty.

They wanted her to go to parenting classes and see a psychologist regularly. We said, "We don't believe in that either, but if that will help you get your child back, why don't you just go there? Close your ears and sit through it."

We should have had more understanding of the fact that it was her life, and not ours. Her way of doing things, and not ours. We should have realized that hers didn't have to be like ours. We should not have been so judgemental and so fixed in our way of doing things. That is really hard. The social service system works by requiring you to follow specific steps, and it was so hard for us to accept that she didn't respect those steps; that she didn't want to play that game.

A house with a safe room

When I first looked at the house where SOS now operates and saw that there were three bedrooms, I thought, "Finally." When we did the needs assessment, what people wanted most, besides being listened to and validated, was a safe place for crises. The number one thing was not an advocacy centre, or housing, or a drop-in, but a safe place to go when they were freaking out.

Moving into this house and realizing that we can use one of the rooms as a small, safe place has been wonderful. We're writing a proposal now; we're going to apply for funding for flexible hours. It will be difficult to convince the government to do this, because they want everything standardized. But we want to be able to provide support when the demand is there. We want this room to be really nice and comfortable, with a bed, so that people who just need to get away from where they are will want to stay here. They may or may not want someone here with them at night. Personally, if it was me staying here, I'd like my peace. I think it will be enough for some people just to have others working here during the day and know no one is going to lock them up, or look down on them, or talk badly about them. If people do want somebody to stay with them, we'll do what we've done in the past: together with the women's centre, we'll organize people who are willing to take turns providing crisis support.

People ask, what if someone comes in who's really angry and wants to hit people? Our answer is that we will give them lots of things they can hit. We'll tell them they can hit things and throw things against the walls in this room, but that they can't hit people.

In our four years of existence, no one has ever been violent at SOS. Once, someone came after me with a butcher knife. And I said, very clearly and calmly, "Put that knife down." And that was it. Of course, in that situation, when someone was standing there with a butcher knife, I didn't feel the same as when someone says, "Do you want a coffee?" But I don't think I was really scared. Rather, I was very, very concentrated. I focussed all my energy on this woman. And I was very clear.

Two days later, this woman did the same thing to some nurse who'd gotten a job doing support work with her. As soon as she saw the knife, the nurse screamed like crazy and ran out the door, without boots or anything, in winter, and went to the neighbours and alarmed the whole neighbourhood.

I believe that staying calm is the most effective way to avert violence.

Life after "coming out"

It's been difficult, at times, being known by everyone as an antipsychiatry activist and having personal information about me publicized. I spoke about myself at an information forum once and the media jumped on it and put private stories about me on the front page of the local paper. But even before that, when I first came to Whitehorse with these ideas, I felt unable to express myself in an effective way. I felt insecure; I felt very alone. I sensed that people were looking at me as a strange person; that I was seen as being out of my mind. At one point, a rumour was spread around that I'd lied about my psychology degree, that I'd made it up.

It's really hard not to question yourself when you're stuck in a small community where many people have such idiotic views. You always feel so different. There have been times when I've gone home after work and cried and cried and cried, and said, "Why am I not like them?" When I thought I'd be a lot happier if I were as ignorant and self-righteous as they were.

I think the biggest turnaround for me was the enormous amount of support I got from Gay Hansen. I felt she lent me some of her power. And having SOS behind me and knowing we've done such good work has made all the difference. Now I'm much more able to express myself and feel that I get my views across.

My connections with people outside the Yukon who are part of the same struggle have been invaluable. It's been so good spending time with people like Carla McKague and Judi Chamberlin and Bonnie Burstow. And going to NARPA [the National Association for Rights Protection and Advocacy, a U.S. organization of advocates for psychiatric patients that holds annual conferences] and feeling part of that; being among people I really respect, and who value me.

Judi Johnny is a board member of the Second Opinion Society. She is chair of Women on Wings, a sister group of the DisAbled Women's Network of

Canada, and serves on the boards of directors of the Victoria Faulkner Women's Centre and the Yukon Status of Women Collective. A long-time crusader for the rights of people with disabilities, Judi is Yukon representative of the National Aboriginal Network on Disabilities. She also belongs to the sixty-country International Coalition of Women With Disabilities and the Feminist Literacy Workers' Network. She has recently "come out" as a psychiatric survivor.

○

Judi Johnny

I invited myself to be part of SOS. Or, rather, I encouraged them to include people who have physical disabilities and have also had psychiatric treatment, and who want to be involved. At that time, I wasn't willing to say that I was a psychiatric survivor. That would mean opening up my book and saying, "This is what I'm like"—making myself vulnerable.

I found out about SOS by word of mouth; I was talking to Gisela. And I felt that there should be more contact with people with disabilities, since they suffer many of the same kinds of oppression psychiatric survivors do. Because of being different, they are put in a special position. So I wanted to make sure that, if the group's focus was applicable to them, people with disabilities would have a chance to be involved. To have the door at least beginning to open. They had a few meetings at my house, and we talked about basics like wheelchair access.

It's the kind of thing people don't want to deal with, disabilities along with psychiatric experience. It's like, if you have both of those together, you must be really nuts. And if you add being a lesbian, it's even more wonderful. It's like people are accusing you. And I say, maybe I am all those things, but the fact is that the system screwed me up.

When I was quite young, I was kept on a psychiatric ward for six months out of the year, just because I was physically disabled. Society wanted me out of sight. They put me with adults with psychiatric problems, which gave me a very perverted idea of adults, right from the start. They figured I'd be okay with these other misfits, because I wasn't completely whole to begin with, and not the right colour or the right gender. It was a convenient place for them to stash me. It seemed as if, because of my disability and my gender and my race, I wasn't even human.

Being on the psychiatric ward helped me in a sense, because that's where I got the "oomph" to fight. I wasn't about to be pushed around. I'm pretty small. Until a few years ago, I was sixty-five pounds soaking wet, and four-foot-nothing. I was just one of these tiny folks. It was like I was a kid all my life. The other patients looked after me.

After this recent bout of having to use the wheelchair again, I've been abused all over again, psychologically, physically and emotionally. I thought maybe it would be a good idea to speak out publicly about psychiatry, because that's where so much abuse comes from. But I've always shied away from speaking to people in the disability community about psychiatric issues. People who talk about such things are shunned for being weird. And in the Native community, psychiatry is seen as a white thing, besides being shameful. However, many Native people have been pushed into the white psychiatric system. Again, we're not fitting in. We're different.

Coming out as a psychiatric survivor has made my life harder, in a way. But it's also made even more of a fighter out of me. I think that once I get the psychiatric issues out of my system, my life will be more normal. I'm not talking about what's normal in the able-ist community, but about what's normal for me. It's time for me to deal with those issues so I can carry on with life and be stronger and more politically active than I am now. This is a comfortable time for me to acknowledge that part of my life. To say, "This has happened to me, and it's part of why I'm the way I am now. I don't care if you accept me any better or any worse; this is where I am now. I have nothing to lose."

People say to me, "How is it that a disabled woman can have the energy to do this?" What a dumb question!

What I've found in the psychiatric survivors' movement is that people become better fighters, rather than being submissive. We are stronger fighters, and we're determined to get past the people who are trying to keep us down. And to do it without having to conform to society. When you look at people who do conform, frankly, they're weirder than we are. And they're accepted. They've got credentials for their stupidity.

Because SOS is a close-knit group and I already know the people in it, it's easy for me to talk to them. At SOS, you can make a mistake and nobody criticizes you. You can be what you are and not be judged. Everybody is in the same boat. You get days when you see somebody else in a bad situation; other times they see you in a bad situation. You're accepted as equal; people understand that there's nothing wrong with you.

People who are labelled as having psychiatric problems have a special quality. Often we are more spiritual and more humane. These may be qualities that we've acquired, or they may have been given to us by the Creator or the goddess or whoever we talk to. For some crazy reason, these seem to be qualities that society can't handle. We're not allowed to try and deal with our feelings. Instead, they psychiatrize us and make things worse. We have to be able to say, "Hey, you're messing with my spirit. And my spirit doesn't like it."

I'd like to see the movement come up with alternatives to the so-called treatments that the system offers. I'd like looking weird and being weird to become acceptable. There's nothing wrong with not being whatever the norm is. Whose norm is it, anyway?

I want to see the movement educate society as a whole about the fact that there's nothing wrong with us and the fact that we are not "consumers" of "services." We didn't have a choice to go in and say, "Hey, I wouldn't mind some electroshock treatment. I wouldn't mind those pills. I wouldn't mind you calling me down like I was a piece of shit." We didn't ask for that. It's not my fault that I was born a First Nations woman with a disability. I got psychiatrized because I was different and, later, because I dared to speak my mind. It's another process of genocide. First the missionaries, then the residential schools, and now, psychiatrists.

I'd like to see a place where you could get good counselling if that's what you wanted. Feminists should be able to have feminist counsellors. The same should be true for Native women or women with disabilities. Or if, like myself, you don't fit into any one box but fall into a lot of different categories, you should be able to pick and choose what you want. The important thing is that you're treated as a human being by someone who can really understand what you're talking about.

Traditional healing for emotional trouble

When I was young, I used to see people who would be considered, in white people's terms, to have psychiatric problems, who were given herbs and being counselled by the elders. So I knew right from the start that, no matter what was wrong in your life, it could be healed. I have my own medicine bag that I use for different things.

But Native people have been taught from day one how to use those things and where to go. I've seen too many people misuse parts of other people's cultures for their own benefit. The thing to understand is that it's not about your personal needs; in the long run, you're doing this to benefit the community. And if you misuse somebody else's culture, even if it's innocent, it's detrimental.

Now, if you, as a non-Native person who was having emotional problems, heard that someone else with similar problems had been helped by going to a sweat lodge, you could go to whoever you heard that from and say, "I would like to try that." But you have to acknowledge and respect the culture this practice comes from. A lot of people try to use it without acknowledging or respecting it. And then it doesn't work.

Links between oppressed groups

I think some members of psychiatric survivors' groups need to join up with other groups, like Native and disability groups, if only as honorary members. I think psychiatric survivors should be coming to us and saying, "We'd love you to be part of our group. This is what we're doing, and we respect what you're doing. I think we have similarities; we're fighting the same people." Eventually, when there's enough support and trust, maybe a few people from that group will open up and say, "This is what happened to me, and I see where your group is going to be help-ful to me."

I had a group of my own for disabled women, but I also joined the Yukon Sta-tus of Women Collective. I think it would be okay if a group of Native survivors formed and joined SOS, but as a subgroup, maybe having a member on the board. But that would be it, until we became more comfortable.

The thing is, it's not Natives looking for other Native people; it's the white people in SOS. But right now, I think it's too much of a burden on me to go and look for psychiatric survivors in my own community when I'm not really well accepted because of my disability. But just the fact that SOS has one person there who's Native is enough for now. It's token, yes, and I accept that. You have to start somewhere. But they shouldn't expect that one Native person to find others. They, as survivors, should take the initiative and look for people and say, "Would you like to be part of our group? So far, we have only one member who's Native."

Irit told me that she was once asked to speak at a conference of people with disabilities and refused on the grounds that she wasn't disabled and didn't want to encourage the idea that "mental illness" was a disability. I think that's pom-pous. Maybe they don't have another person in that group who'll talk about those things. They need someone from outside to come in and say something about psychiatry. To sow that seed and then step aside, and let the people in the group take it upon themselves to go on from there.

Maybe you don't feel you belong to the disabled group. But you could try saying, "I have been labelled as having a psychiatric disability. I don't think there's any such thing. I was disabled by the medications; let me talk to you about that." Then you can reach into that group. Even though you might not have a disability, there may be people who do and who want to be part of your group. So you want to be able to give an opening to someone who has a disability, who doesn't fit into the disability community for some reason—psychiatric or whatever. And you should remember that a lot of people with other issues don't feel they have a disability but have been labelled as having one.

Susan Marshall lives out in the country in northwestern Ontario. Brand new to political organizing when she was hired by OPSA, Susan travelled to several towns in her area and started psychiatric survivors' groups in all of them. The network of groups she founded, originally called the Sunset Country chapter of OPSA, was one of the strongest parts of OPSA and has continued after OPSA folded. The groups there had a profound effect on both how people were treated in hospital and how they felt about themselves.

Susan Marshall

Our group has done some pretty serious advocacy work. One woman had a three-month freakout. We rallied around her. It was so powerful, thinking, "I'm not going to let this get as bad for you as it was for me." And we kept her out of the hospital.

Her kids were telling her to grow up, snap out of it. And she felt guilty because she couldn't. The doctor had prescribed Luvox (an antidepressant). She refused it. She was determined not to go into the hospital. I said, "Talk to your doctor and give me a call if things get rough." And, sure enough, they did. She called and told me she couldn't handle it.

I picked her up. The main thing I kept saying was, "I've been through this and I made it, and so will you." I organized two people from the group and also the people who run Nelson House, which used to be a group home for people coming out of institutions. After we pressured them, it expanded into a crisis house. It's as close to a safe house as you can get, considering it's staffed by professionals. They're young social workers and very caring. Anyway, we decided we'd take care of her for three months. The most frustrating thing is knowing that all a person needs is your support to get through this, but that you can't be on for twenty-four hours a day, and that there aren't enough of you available.

It was a long three months. She would disappear, hide in boxes under the stairs in the basement. She was afraid to sleep. She was convinced she had to stay awake to fight what was going on. All we did was say, "You're going to make it through this." It helped to be able to say that we had been through very similar experiences. Sometimes she heard noises that scared her and she'd say, "Oh my god, what's that? The world's going to end!" And we'd just say, "No, it's not." A cop car would go by and she'd say, "They're coming to get me!" We would tell her they weren't. And that would help. Whereas I think if she'd been alone, she would have continued freaking.

Once in a while she'd want to go into the hospital, and we'd convince the doctor to let her stay in a local hospital rather than ship her off to another town. We convinced Nelson House to take her when she was afraid to be alone.

We ran interference between her and her family. Her daughter would yell at her, "Just make up your mind to change!" We'd yell back. We'd say she'd get over this. She'd come back; we knew, because we had. We'd spend time listening to the family and talking to them. When she freaked out and felt afraid of her sister, we'd tell the sister she didn't want to see her that day. When she did want to see her and the sister got started on a topic that made her upset, we'd say that wasn't a good subject to discuss.

It was totally made up. We didn't know what we were doing. But we kept telling her she wouldn't be sent away. That was her worst fear.

She had a good counsellor, but that was only for two hours a week.

At one point she decided to go to the hospital because she couldn't sleep. She asked me to go with her. Thank god I did, because she got a real jackass of a doctor. I demanded another one, and we got one. This guy listened. When she couldn't talk, I took over. She got a prescription for something to help her sleep. The first doctor said she was psychotic and wanted to put her on chlorpromazine (a neuroleptic). She would have taken anything, but I said, "No. That's not an option."

She was quite willing to take any medication. We'd give her information about the drugs she was being offered. They'd try one drug after another, like she was a guinea pig. One of the drugs made her act really weird; they took her off that one.

She was hospitalized for about a month at one point. Quite a few of us were there whenever she wanted us, almost twenty-four hours a day.

At one point she was really clinging to us. It had been a month, and we were really tired. But we had each other to bitch and complain to when the going got rough. Our goal remained to keep her where she wanted to be and to make it easier for her to go through this.

Gradually, it came to an end. She became able to sleep. Then we only went to the hospital at night. Eventually, she didn't want us there.

The day that things started changing for her, I had been totally frustrated. She was in the "woe-is-me" syndrome: "I feel dead inside, I can't leave the house, I can never work again" (she had had a job as a hairdresser). I was at the end of my rope. I went to a social worker friend and said, "What can we do here? What would you do?" I knew he wouldn't tell anyone about any of this. He sat and brainstormed with me and then said, "Maybe what she needs to know is that she can still work."

I told her that everyone at the clubhouse would love a haircut, but no one could afford it. She was terrified, but said, "Yes. I can do it." She hadn't left her house for some time. The first time we tried it, she cancelled. She couldn't leave the house. The second time, she made it to the clubhouse. And it worked! As soon as she'd done one haircut, she knew she was capable of working again.

As corny as this sounds, I think what made it work was us having faith in her, having confidence that she could do it. And because she wasn't being paid, it didn't seem like it would be so terrible if she screwed up. But she did it well and felt proud of herself. That day, it turned around for her because we pushed it, and the whole community rallied around her. Now, she has her own life back. But it was a pretty intense time.

Last time she'd had this kind of trouble, she'd been sent to a hospital in another town for eighteen months. She was catatonic for most of it. This time, the whole experience lasted five months; three that were very intense, and two that were less intense.

We made one mistake—she would never say she didn't like something, and we were trying everything. One of us was taking her for walks down to the beach to watch the seagulls. When she was getting better, she told us how much she hated those seagulls.

But knowing we'd saved her from being sent away was a real high, especially because many people in the group had been through getting sent away themselves. Now she's getting along with her daughters, going bowling, doing her thing. She doesn't need us anymore, except as friends.

Being able to help this woman was a powerful thing. And we didn't see ourselves as her saviours. We helped improve her situation, but we didn't need her to stay dependent on us. Every step she took away from us was a pleasure. That's one way in which what we did was so different from psychiatry.

It was exhausting, though, especially since we had to keep working all through this time.

So that's a story with a happy ending. Now I'll tell you another story.

Two years ago, a member of our group called. She lives in a housing complex for people with disabilities. They have support staff who call us in to attend case conferences if people aren't willing to show up on their own, so we can advocate for them or just be there with them.

This woman hadn't left her apartment in seven months. Before that, she'd been seen walking down the hall naked. Flies were coming out of her apartment. There was no food going in. Her mail hadn't been picked up. She wouldn't let anyone in. She'd gotten rid of all her furniture. She'd started a fire in the microwave. She'd been off her medications and was doing things they called psychotic. She'd been diagnosed schizophrenic.

The doctor said she had to be committed. She wasn't eating or taking care of herself. They called me to be there for the committal. The doctor said he'd send an ambulance the next day. I said I'd try to talk her into coming to the hospital first.

The next day, a cop came to the door. The ambulance was outside. I said, "We agreed that I'd get to talk to her first."

When we went in, there were flies everywhere. She was sitting there eating her own shit. She was right out of it. The person I knew just wasn't there. I tried to talk her into going to the hospital, but she wouldn't. The cop and the ambulance driver took her. We convinced the hospital staff, with difficulty, to let us into her room when they took her in. We sat and tried to talk to her.

She was convinced they'd been called because her apartment was a mess. Actually, everyone was concerned that she was dying. She'd lost a lot of weight.

She was taken to Lakehead Psychiatric Hospital [the provincial hospital in Thunder Bay, hundreds of kilometres from this woman's home town]. I explained to her that she had no rights until she was "formed" [this refers to a certificate being filled out which clarifies your status in the hospital: it specifies that you've been committed, and for how long]. She wanted a lawyer. I explained she couldn't have one until she'd been assessed. You can't challenge the form until after they assess you.

If you live in a big city, it might be a half-hour ride to the hospital. Here, they transport you six hours away and then dump you in a strange town.

So, she went off to Lakehead. They put her back on medications, and it was like night and day. She was back to herself. I thought, "She'll be furious. She'll blame me. I shouldn't have done this."

She told me afterwards that she was really grateful and wished people hadn't let the situation go for so long. She said that if she ever went back off her medications, she wished people would do something about it sooner, so she wouldn't lose her dignity.

A year later, she again decided she didn't need the medications. She started withdrawing, talking about holes in her face and body. She thought everyone was out to get her and that her phone was tapped. She thought there was stuff coming over the phone lines into holes in her face.

Her case worker wrote a note to her doctor, who decided to "form" her and send her to Lakehead. He told her she'd be formed two days later. They called and told me about it—I'd tried all along to keep contact. I asked if there was anything I could do. She let me in and asked if I knew what was going to happen. I told her that they were coming to get her, and that there was nothing I could do about it. As far as the doctor was concerned, she had to take her medications or she'd be formed and taken away. Those were the options. I asked her what she wanted to do.

Her place was pretty gross, but not as bad as before. She said, "I'll clean the place up. I'll start eating better." I replied, "That's not what this is about." She agreed to take the medications. We went to the clinic and I asked if she'd like me to come into the consulting room with her. She said no, I should send the social worker in. So I did.

The doctor asked how I got her to come in. "It's really quite simple," I said, "I told her she had a choice between medications and hospital. That's all she had, right?"

She chose to take pills instead of shots, and I took her back to her apartment. She said, "I bet you think you're some kind of fucking saint. You think you saved me. I know you do."

I felt like the biggest shit that ever lived.

Now she's back to her old self. She'll talk to me, but there's something there between us. I feel it. I've said to her, "Did I do the right thing?" And she won't say.

She's brilliant. I have a painting of hers on my bedroom wall. She's so talented! But because her reality, even with the medications, is so different from everyone else's, she can't get a job. She can't be accepted. And I think she thinks, "Why is life worth living like this? Why not escape into a different reality?"

When you see someone come back to your version of reality with medications, you wonder why they ever go off. But she thinks the medications pollute her body. That was the only thing she ever told me about it that made any sense to me.

The point is, why the hell could she be blackmailed like that? That guy could "form" her because he wanted to. The law says that if you're a serious threat to yourself or others, or can't take care of yourself, they can commit you. But she hadn't reached that point, that time.

When you lose touch with what we call reality, you can't affect the system, no matter how intelligent you are. The only ones who can change it are those who can masquerade as being as "normal" as other people. The real changes this woman needs are beyond my comprehension, and she can't or won't say what they are.

I often think that whatever's supposed to be "wrong" with us is just our way of coping with the crap we go through. If you end up with a psychiatrist, they medicalize you. If you end up with someone who cares and tells you you'll get through it, then you will.

I was diagnosed manic depressive and taught that that was something I couldn't control. I was real pissed off when my counsellor suggested that maybe it was something I *could* control. One time I told him I couldn't go home. My husband had told me that if I didn't act normal he'd have me committed. I couldn't act normal. So my counsellor said, "Stay somewhere else." I wanted to be sent home or to have my hand held. But I stayed away. And it was okay.

I've learned that I'm strong enough to get a lot done, as long as I remember to take time off and put myself first. If I'm not okay, I can't do anything for anyone else. And the other thing is to know what you're good at. Our movement needs to accept and appreciate individuals' talents without expecting them to be able to do everything. You need all the separate pieces, and people, to make it work.

Making connections

Because I was part of OPSA, people thought I was antipsychiatry, and there was a lot of anger about that. But I found that because we welcomed people to the group no matter what their views were, the neatest things started to happen. If you respect what people think, they'll listen to you.

One guy came in here who's had hundreds of electroshocks. He holds the record for number of admissions at the local hospital. He's been on every kind of drug. And he's the neatest guy you'd ever want to meet. When we first met him, he thought the system was wonderful. Then he got more and more involved here. We had information available, both pro and con, about ECT and drugs. Now he's totally off medications and suing his psychiatrist! With our help, he got legal aid to take his case on. There are two suits. One is about the shock treatment—he was never given the opportunity to give informed consent. Then, they didn't revoke his driver's licence when he was on so much medication. So he's suing for incompetence. He's been off drugs for more than a year. And he's not drinking, either. Now he figures he isn't crazy and never was.

If he'd gone to the provincial organization and said he loved drugs, shock and his shrink, he'd have been laughed out. But here, with everyone, including him, discussing their experiences, he changed his mind on his own.

The leaders of OPSA wanted the organization to be just for people who identified themselves as psychiatric survivors. But if consumers aren't welcome, what you end up with is a little group of rabid people yelling and affecting nothing. Like it or not, psychiatry's got the power right now.

And here in Fort Frances, we've known all along that not all mental health workers are against us. The CMHA is one of the reasons that our group exists. Specifically, Sheila Shaw [executive director of the local CMHA] wrote our funding proposal. The CMHA supported us by offering free clerical services, copying and mailing. They helped us hire staff and get space. And Sheila supported me personally. She had faith in me. For someone who is "normal" to have faith that I'll pull through when I'm suicidal is phenomenal. She is an amazing lady.

We're also aware that the bureaucrats aren't all against us. My first experience of Bev Lever [then director of the community mental health branch of the Ministry of Health] was at Rising Tide, OPSA's provincial conference. She was a very impressive speaker. I didn't realize at that time who she was or what power she had. I next met her at the Minaki conference. She came at my suggestion. She was really impressive there. Really human.

Everyone was so nervous that she was coming. And it felt neat, her coming to see us, rather than one or two of us going to Toronto to see her. She called and asked if it was okay if she wore jeans and sneakers! I said, "What else would you wear?" I drove her around the region. She talked to me about how much she believed in the movement and how much she was counting on the survival of the provincial office. About how much the movement meant to her.

We met with psychiatric survivors and service providers in Kenora [one of the towns with a group that was part of the network]. The service providers were all in three-piece suits. Bev sat on a couch with some survivors. I was standing at the front with the providers. They started whispering: "Does anyone know if Bev Lever is here?" "I don't know. What does she look like?" "I don't know." I'd planned to introduce her right away, but as soon as I heard that, I decided not to.

We had lunch. People kept whispering, "Do you think she's here yet?" "Where is she?" Afterwards, I told her what had happened. She loved it.

She was a really great lady. I don't know if she had the purest motives, and I don't really care. She liked coming here, and she made herself real to us.

The movement in northwestern Ontario

The movement isn't organized. But to me, if things are moving in a direction, there's a movement. At first, you can't recognize it. But even though it looks really small, things are changing. That's a movement. Someone has moved an idea to the point where it's possible.

A hundred and forty people in northwestern Ontario are willing to admit they've been diagnosed as crazy. They're willing to tell their neighbours. I walk into the doughnut shop, and there's a whole table of crazy people who'll tell other people where they've been and what they've done. That never would have happened ten years ago. Never. There's a lot more acceptance of us than there used to be.

In Kenora, we meet officially with hospital staff four times a year. (We meet with them socially about that often, on other occasions.) The first time we met, they accepted a suggestion about changing the ugly curtains in the hospital. The second time, they accepted a suggestion about not locking down the wards after eight.

Before we came in, people had to earn the "privilege" of being allowed to wear their own clothes. We got rid of that. The staff no longer waits for lawyers to give rights advice. They tell patients about their rights themselves. We've established a relationship: they can tell us their problems and we can tell them ours.

There's another thing, too: in Kenora, close to one-third of the staff have admitted that they've had psychiatric treatment. If we hadn't been there talking about it, they never would have admitted it. One nurse told us about herself, and then suddenly other people felt safe enough to talk about it in our presence. Some even admit to their patients now that they've been psychiatrized. And they've talked to us about the risks involved in doing that.

They have problems in their work. Legally, they have to have a shrink on duty. But what we've got here are fly-in docs. One on Monday, one on Tuesday and one on Thursday. Or one for three days, and then the next week another one for three days. It drives people wacko to have to tell their stories over and over. Some of the doctors are good, but some are awful.

Sometimes what the staff wants to do clashes with what they're required to do. Sometimes a doctor says that a certain patient must have a certain medication, and they disagree. We've worked on ways of dealing with that. Let's say a patient is on one drug one week and then a new doctor comes in and puts him or her on a different drug the next week. The staff will often object. They can chart their objection, but it's a hell of a risk. The doctor could call them on it, saying they don't have the necessary expertise. So they've invented different ways of telling the patient that this might not be what's best and that he or she has the right to consent or refuse.

There have been complaints about certain staff members by others. And now they're starting to be willing to confront each other and back up the complaints.

A lot has changed, and the only reason that what's happening here ever got started is because of OPSA. No one can ever take that away. These communities in the northwest were very closed. I was like everyone else here: I didn't admit my history to anyone. I sure as hell wasn't proud of it.

In our first year, the help of the provincial office was vital. Then, as it started to break up, we got strong enough to exist on our own. We never could have made it without that initial connection, though.

FOUR

HOPE

O

The Canadian mad movement started changing people's lives for the better long before I got involved. Only a few of its accomplishments have made it into this book. In the early 1970s in Vancouver, some of the same people who were involved with the Mental Patients Association, along with others, founded the Vancouver Emotional Emergency Centre (VEEC). VEEC was a drug-free (and that included psychiatric drugs!) alternative to going to the hospital for people in crisis. Its staff and volunteers, some of whom had originally come to the house for help, used techniques like yoga and good nutrition instead of psychiatric treatments. But what really worked at VEEC was friendship, mutual respect and nonjudgemental discussion, both among residents and between them and workers. VEEC was funded for only two years, but was wildly successful while it lasted and could still provide a model for similar efforts.

In 1982, Vancouver artist and author Persimmon Blackbridge, together with her friend, ex-psychiatric inmate Sheila Gilhooly, created *Still Sane*—a document of Sheila's experiences in the mental health system, where drugs and electroshock were used in an unsuccessful attempt to cure her of lesbianism. *Still Sane* started out as a sculpture exhibition and had further incarnations as a video and as a book. (The book was published by Press Gang Publishers, who had previously published *Women Look at Psychiatry* in 1975 and *The Anti-Psychiatry Bibliography and Resource Guide* in 1979, both now out of print.) People across Canada saw and/or read *Still Sane*, and many got clued in about psychiatry as a result.

Mad movement activists in this country have started self-help, political and creative groups that have made a real difference. We have produced and distributed literature that lays out in accessible language the information patients need—and don't get from their psychiatrists—about the drugs they are given. We have done effective advocacy both inside and outside psychiatric facilities. We have changed mental health legislation, won compensation for victims of psychiatric abuse and played key roles in court cases involving crazy people. We have developed convincing arguments about the nonexistence of mental illness, psychiatry as social control, psychiatric drugs as chemical straitjackets, psychiatry's inability to predict dangerousness, and how the community mental health system infantilizes people. We have put out information about all this and more, using every kind of medium imaginable. We have protested against psychiatric abuses and launched lawsuits. We have begun to integrate our movement with other social movements, such as the movement for the rights of people with disabilities. We have helped people stay out of hospital. We have taken the focus off the defects of those who've been through the mental health system and put it on their strengths. We have had enough impact to produce outraged resistance from the mental health establishment.

Looking at all this, I've come to the conclusion that the mad movement in this country, though not united, is present and powerful. The question now is how it can be made stronger. Clearly, its members need ways of communicating with each other. We need to do more to educate the public about how psychiatry hurts people. I believe that, to do this effectively, we must offer viable alternatives. We're not likely to abolish psychiatry. But wouldn't it be wonderful if we could establish a whole range of other options and then let people vote with their feet?

There is no single alternative for people who experience what psychiatry calls mental illness. Different things will work for different people (which is one of the things psychiatry fails to recognize). But people have tried many things that work. For example, people in communes, cooperative houses and families have made their homes safe places where those who are in trouble can be treated well and not interfered with.

Les frères et soeurs (reprise)

Les frères et soeurs d'Emile Nelligan, in Montreal, talked to me about why it is necessary, now more than ever, to build a strong alternatives movement. Increased lobbying by family organizations in favour of confinement and forcible drugging makes it essential that advocates for the human rights of mental patients speak up. Les frères et soeurs also stressed the need for a perspective that does not endorse the universal dependence on medications.

> "It makes everything very easy to interpret trouble as sickness. Some groups in the Regroupement [Quebec's "alternatives" coalition] have very medically-oriented therapy programs. They dispense medications to clients. They fear that without them people might commit suicide. They don't help people to become responsible for themselves. There is no criticism of the idea that, if you feel bad, you run to the shrink and he gives you pills. People don't want to denounce the pushers when the drugs are their only crutch."

Les frères et soeurs have a very clear picture of what alternatives should look like. First of all, people need more information when making decisions about treatment and medications; there should be communication networks that provide and exchange such information. Then there should be safe places where people can go and be treated in a nonjudgemental and caring way—places that involve and are driven by the people who use and need them. Holistic ways of reducing stress, such as yoga, acupuncture and diet, need to be taken more seriously. There must be detox programs for getting off psychiatric drugs. And all these alternatives need to exist outside the mental health system:

> "We are talking about training psychiatrized people to provide alternatives, including how to relate to people when they first come in the door of an alternative place. The place should not look like a hospital or emergency service. No one should wear uniforms or any special clothes. People should come and go as they please, and should be greeted with a smile when they come in; attitude is all-important. People can go out casually for coffee or participate in cultural activities together, or just talk."

Outlets for creative expression are vital. Many crazy people paint, write, sculpt, make music. Mad movement activists have encouraged each other to do these things and to find ways of getting the work out into the public (and, ideally, be paid for it). People who experience extremely strong emotions—that is, "the mentally ill"—need to be able to express those emotions, especially when they have been suppressed by psychiatric treatment. It can be tremendously helpful to do this in creative ways—ways that can involve having fun as well as dealing with pain. One of the people who participated in the Puzzle Factory theatre troupe wrote about how that experience affected him:

> "Performance exists within every action. Performance is the coordination of mind and body and face. Perform with discipline and you will find control within life.
>
> "The answer in life lies in the control of your environment. The body is the world of the soul. To discipline the body is to shape your environment at its most basic.
>
> "The stage is an extension of the performer. Model the environment of the stage through the performance, and all the world seems more controllable. I feel safe, for I know my part. I feel safe, for I know that my world is limited to the stage and the audience.
>
> "I feel good, because I am the centre of attention. I feel good, because I am getting the attention that I have always needed but never had the courage to demand."

When things are bad

People have changed their lives by starting and joining groups focussed on fun and creative activity. But that's not the kind of thing you're likely to do when things are bad for you and you're in crisis or feel you can't go on anymore. The mad movement has also come up with ways of helping yourself get through these times. Here are some strategies various people have used:

"If at all possible, I find someone to talk to whom I can trust. I've been able to find people who, if they are around and have time, will talk to me on the phone or even get together with me when I'm in trouble. It helps that they know I'm willing to do the same for them."

"I sometimes go outside, no matter what the weather's like, and walk. Just moving and changing where I am can make a difference."

"I find breathing deeply and standing up straight can help. So can stretching or listening to calming music."

"No matter what kind of shape I'm in, writing about how I'm feeling helps. Doing that for long enough almost always gives me some perspective."

"Having something to eat can make a difference. Sometimes I think it's the end of the world, but it's really just that I'm hungry."

"I resort to screaming, preferably in a place where it won't frighten anyone or get me in trouble. Sometimes I'll hit things or tear things up."

"If I absolutely can't stand the way I feel, I knock myself out with herbal concoctions or, if I don't have anything else, a couple of Gravol. (I know, it's a pharmaceutical drug, but I looked it up, and the side effects are nothing compared to those of psychiatric drugs.)"

"I'm slowly learning to remember that I've felt this bad before, and that it doesn't last forever and doesn't mean there's something dreadfully wrong with me."

If you're locked up

The basic strategy for getting out is to be as calm and cooperative as possible. This does not mean believing that what the doctors and other staff tell you about yourself is right. It's simply a matter of doing what they want you to so that they can see that you're rational and that, according to their beliefs, you want to "get better." Again and again, in the mad movement, in community mental health "clubhouses" I've visited and when I was in hospital, people have used the same words about how to get out: "play the game."

It's virtually impossible to avoid being drugged immediately if you are admitted in the state they call "psychotic," and, unfortunately, for some people this makes the craziness worse. But if you can act like a good patient as soon as you are somewhat able to think again, you should be able to get out relatively quickly, so they won't have time to drug you enough to do extensive damage.

If you are drugged over a longer period, however, it's very important to get off the drugs gradually. People with experience in this area often recommend that you reduce your dose by 10 percent at a time, waiting after each reduction to make sure that your system has adjusted to the lower dose. Eating well and getting some exercise and a lot of rest are vital during withdrawal, and so is getting as much support as possible from people you can trust. Anything you know of that makes you feel good and that is not bad for your health is a good thing to get a lot of at this time.

Helping someone else

What can you do for someone who is having a severe freakout? When I summarized what people recommended and what they thought should be avoided, it boiled down to doing the opposite of what the mental health system does:

- Don't panic. Stay calm and be confident that the freakout will end.
- Don't use force. The natural reaction if you do will be terror and rage. Instead, be gentle and respectful.
- Don't assume or tell the person that this is happening because they're sick.

Assume and tell them that the freakout is temporary and that they're going to be okay.

- Don't dismiss the person's "delusions." Listen respectfully if they want to talk, even if what they're saying doesn't make sense to you. Whatever they're on about, however strange, may be a clue to how you can help them get what they need. They may want some understanding about how they feel, as well as reassurance that no one is going to force "treatment"—or anything else—on them.

- Don't withhold information from, mislead or lie to someone in the belief that you are "protecting" them. Otherwise you are not being trustworthy.

- Don't take away people's choices. Offer more choices. Ask if they have any ideas about what they need right now. Talk about what's helped you when you're freaking out. You may want to make suggestions such as, "Do you want something to eat? Do you want to lie down? Do you want to go for a walk? Do you want to be alone? Do you want a hug?"

- Don't be mean. Don't be cold. Be kind and helpful and careful and thoughtful. But don't infantilize or patronize. Don't make assumptions about what people want or need. Always try to find out by asking. This includes asking whether and when they want you around.

- Don't push tranquillizers. Understand that people who are freaking out may need the full use of their mental faculties in order to cope both with being upset and with whatever caused them to become upset.

- Don't shut the person up in another room. Isolation, loneliness, helplessness and feelings of being persecuted are very often contributing factors in a freakout.

- Don't feed people lousy, starchy food and lots of sugar, meat and coffee unless that's what they particularly want. Offer different kinds of food, including food that's likely to help people calm down and feel better, like whole grains (which have lots of B Vitamins—good for the nerves). And make sure it's tasty!

- Don't think you're a big deal because you're helping. Remember that you may need the same kind of help some day.

People generally advised that if you feel you have to take someone to the hospital, you should tell the person what you're doing and why. Try to stay with the person through the admission process, be around as much as possible afterwards, and do what you can to help him or her get out quickly.

What we need when we're out in the world

Besides alternatives to hospital treatment in the case of crisis, people in the mad movement—and some people who have never heard of the mad movement but understand what some of the problems are—have been working on alternatives to the "community mental health" system. This system has been put in place to meet our "special needs" after we come home from the hospital. Besides continuing to see psychiatrists and take drugs, we're supposed to need supportive housing or other residential facilities, day programs, and vocational and psychosocial rehabilitation. But what if we'd rather have homes, jobs and friends?

> "We need support, love, human contact—the same things everyone else needs. Opportunities. Experiences. Once you become institutionalized, you go into a shell. Once you have opportunities again, you blossom."

> "We need to be able to make money, like anyone else. The government encourages us to be invalids. People who want disability benefits are stuffing the pills down, saying 'Am I sick enough yet?' If you're declared incapable of working you can still dream, but the means of making your dreams come true are knocked out from under you. People feel trapped into not wanting to feel better so they won't lose disability benefits."

News stories about mental patients who are poor and homeless imply that their "disease" is at fault. But try getting a job or renting an apartment when your tongue constantly darts in and out of your mouth or you can't stop twitching or making chewing motions because of tardive dyskinesia—the very common neurological disease caused by "antipsychotic medications." With drugs, electroshock, intimidation, coercion, humiliation—and of course, with the best of intentions—the mental health system has created a subclass of sick, unemployable, unhappy people—chronic mental patients.

People who have been made into mental patients (and those who might be, which is everyone else) need to find ways of making their worlds saner places. The possibilities are infinite. One that I know of has been realized right here in Canada. Its focus is one of the things the "chronic mental patients" I've talked with want most: real work.

In June 1996 I discovered, to my astonishment, that there's something going on in this country on behalf of mental patients that wasn't started by mental patients but that actually makes sense. I have long had a fantasy about starting a funny farm out in the country. When I heard about Providence Farm, I was eager to check it out.

The property consists of 400 acres, 330 of them forested, on Vancouver Island, a few kilometres east of a town called Duncan. It's leased from the Sisters of Saint Anne, a teaching and nursing order of Catholic nuns who have owned it since 1863. It's a beautiful place.

The staff I met were Christine Winter and Jack Hutton. I assumed Christine came from a mental health background, and was surprised when she told me her degree was in agriculture. Jack is a psychiatric social worker, but not, said Christine, by any means a typical one. He relies on empathy and common sense, rather than information gleaned from textbooks. Jack and Christine referred to the people they're there for as workers—not "clients" or "consumers."

The workers get training and experience in baking; pottery; woodworking; lapidary; sewing; small motor repairs; shearing, spinning and carding wool; making felt products (there are six sheep on the farm); and growing food and other plants. They all get minimum wage. These are people who may previously have been employed in sheltered workshops (picture a big room where you sit around with other mental patients tying wires around pieces of plastic for four hours, make four dollars and then go home).

The tour

I went to Providence Farm with a group of people, mostly parents of people labelled schizophrenic, who were interested in creating something similar in the Vancouver area. Jack and Christine gave us a tour (given enough notice, they'll give tours to anyone who asks). They explained that the farm is not a "residential facility." No one lives there; people come there to work. The workers all live in Duncan; they travel to the farm by bike, bus or car; some hitchhike. A local group home sends people in a van. We saw people working outdoors, in the shop and in the kitchen. We were shown the gorgeous public garden, the orchard and the new gazebo. Both workers and visitors were encouraged to "graze" in the garden during our visit; good nutrition is both talked about and practised at the farm.

The program now in place at Providence Farm was started in 1979 in order to create work and activities for people whose needs were met neither in the community nor in the system. Workers who arrive at the farm are not asked "What's your problem?" or "What's your diagnosis?" Rather, they are asked, "What are your abilities? What are you good at? What do you want to learn? What do you want to do?"

Gradually, the program began to provide paid work. These days, there are all kinds of activities that benefit the whole community and raise revenues for the farm. One of the buildings is rented out as an alternative school for kids. There is a popular horseback-riding program for people labelled as having various kinds of disabilities. There's also a seniors' gardening program: there are huge planters up high enough that gardeners needn't bend. "There are other gardening programs for seniors in Duncan," Christine told me, "but only for those who are living in a facility. The farm helps people stay out of places like that longer."

Five hundred people a week use Providence Farm, not including volunteers. They range in age from five to ninety, approximately, and come from all walks of life. There are workers who have been labelled mentally ill, developmentally handicapped, and/or addicted to drugs or alcohol. People who have committed minor crimes have done community service hours at the farm.

The farm receives funding from three branches of the B.C. government: the Ministry of Social Services; the Ministry of Health; and the Ministry of Skills, Training and Education. They also generate an impressive amount of money through produce sales and fund raising. They sold $25,000 worth of nursery stock in 1996. They have hosted the Vancouver Island Folk Festival and other major musical events. A hoe-down held last year netted $12,000. They make $50,000 per year from bingo.

The Greenways Supported Employment Program, located at the farm since 1984, gets half of its funds from Mental Health, a quarter from bingo and the remaining quarter from nursery-stock sales. This is the program under which former psychiatric patients are hired.

Workers at the farm tend to bloom in many ways. Christine told me about a fifty-seven-year-old woman who, when she arrived, was only able to move dirt one shovelful at a time. Now she can push a full wheelbarrow.

Another worker came from a horribly abusive background. When he arrived, it was hard for him to know what love and nurturing were about. He persuaded the staff to get twelve chickens for the farm. He was present when the first egg was laid and carried it tenderly to the people he was working with, as proud and jubilant as a new father. He was also present when a ewe was about to give birth. He helped pull out a stillborn lamb. Before he had much time to react it became clear that there was another lamb, and he helped that one come out. She lived, and he couldn't get over having helped save her. He said she should be called "Lucky," and she was. This man's love of animals and his interactions with them gave him something to talk about, and he ended up being able to relate much more easily to people.

Recently, Providence Farm staff did a survey of people who have worked there over the past ten years, including those working there now. Two-thirds of them have gotten jobs, gone to college and/or entered successful relationships, and have either never been back in a psychiatric facility or have had infrequent, short, voluntary stays. The remaining third, almost without exception, were people with "dual diagnoses"—those whom the system has deemed to be suffering from both "mental illness" and the "disease" of addiction.

People in the area are excited about the farm, which has had excellent publicity in local papers. A nearby nursery donated a thousand dollars' worth of plants to start the public garden. A nearby college and many other institutions (pardon the expression) have made donations. A lumber company allows farm workers to cut firewood for free and sell it at market prices. The money is used to buy equipment.

"It's hard," says Jack, "for some professionals to accept that this is good stuff we're doing here. They feel that we should be sitting in an office talking to people. They don't recognize the value of work and how people need to be valued through their work."

Although Greenways is seen by funders as a therapeutic work program, "the word therapeutic," says Christine, "should not be part of the language we use. We're not caregivers. We're the managers of a small business. We give technical advice. We look at the talents, skills and abilities of our employees. Since they're the ones who do the work, they naturally have a say in how the business is run. At first people come to business meetings and say, 'Why are you asking me how to do this? Isn't that *your* job?' And we say, 'Not any more.' "

In the course of figuring out how to make the business work better and talking about how to describe it to the public, people learn how much things cost, how to use time effectively, how to work with other people, how to present themselves. And work, says Christine, gives people a purposeful routine: "It's really basic stuff."

One worker, a former inmate of Riverview (Vancouver's provincial psychiatric hospital), arrived at the farm and turned out to have computer programming skills. As a result, there is now a computer centre on site. He does all the farm's signs, brochures, pamphlets, letters and sales reconciliations. "I'm computer illiterate myself," says Christine, "and I plan to stay that way."

The staff is constantly shifting responsibility onto the workers. Christine's dream is that the farm be run entirely by the workers: "Our job is to work ourselves out of a job." My ears just about fell off when she said this. I was sharply drawn back to a talk Randy Pritchard and I gave to a group of community mental health workers in the early days of OPSA. Randy fixed the audience with a steely gaze and told them that their job was to work themselves out of a job. They were not impressed. And here was someone being paid to work with mental patients who has figured this out for herself and is willing to say it in public! "Treating people the way you want to be treated is what keeps you on track," Christine told me. How obvious. How unheard of in the area of "mental health."

Graduating from welfare

During the tour we all stopped and sat down in the big, comfortable kitchen for a rest. A worker we'd seen earlier at his job came in and announced, "Guess what? Today is Welfare Wednesday, and thanks to Greenways and Work Warriors, it's the first time I didn't get a cheque. Isn't that nice? I've graduated from welfare." Work Warriors is an entrepreneurship/self-employment workers' cooperative that does general contracting and was initiated by workers at the farm: "We networked throughout the community. Before we even got our business cards printed we lined up six jobs. The government loves it; our welfare workers love it." He obviously loved it too.

Looking for a fly in the ointment, I said to a young woman working in the kitchen, "This place seems perfect, as far as I can tell. But you work here. Do you think it's perfect?" "It's really good," she told me seriously. "They encourage you to go back to college and upgrade your skills if you want to." She clearly thought this was a great idea. So did I.

I told Christine later on that in coming to the farm, I felt as if I had walked over a threshold into a different, better universe. She said a lot of people felt that way.

Providence Farm gives people who have been acted upon by the system for years a chance to act upon the world; to take control of their own lives. And that is the very essence of an alternative to psychiatry.

Communication

Information about projects like Providence Farm should be readily available so that other people can start similar things in their parts of the country. The more mad movement activists talk to each other (whether in person or otherwise), the more ideas and ways of thinking we have access to, the faster we can figure out how to solve the problems we face. The technology that's been developed in the last twenty years has given political movements more ability to network and communicate. Newsletters have become easy to produce as more and more people acquire personal computers and desktop publishing programs, and the Internet is providing increasingly accessible and user-friendly means of communication..

One of the impressive manifestations of the international mad movement is an Internet "mailing list" (discussion group) called *Madness*, which comes out of the United States. Sylvia Caras, the coordinator, says: "*Madness* is an electronic action and information discussion list that convenes people who experience mood swings, fright, voices and visions. *Madness* creates an electronic forum and distribution device for exchanging ways to change social systems, and for distributing any information and resources that might be useful. A basic premise of science and research is also a value of *Madness*: to share your findings with others."

Madness and related mailing lists provide information about topics ranging from herbal alternatives to psychiatric drugs to ways in which people can fight abuses perpetrated by the system. Successes are celebrated, strategies devised and problems discussed and sometimes solved. There's lots of dissent, lots of support and a constant flow of facts and ideas.

The Internet can be used in many ways, not least as an antidote to political and social isolation. It's wonderful for people needing to know something quickly; in writing this book, I e-mailed several mad movement activists I'd "met" on *Madness*, and they helped me fill in some blanks.

I want to see the Canadian movement use the Internet more. But everyone I interviewed for this book agreed that there must also be a national publication through which we can communicate with each other and educate the public, and by means of which the computerless can get information on paper. A magazine like *Phoenix Rising* can be a powerful organizing and fundraising tool.

Rage

Looking back, I feel that one of the things that lessened the impact of *Phoenix* was its constant tone of righteous rage. I've spent many years being furious about psychiatry and yelling about it, and I know I'm going to do that periodically for the rest of my life. I can't help it: the rage is justified by the stories I keep hearing. And it's not just what happens to people once they're inside that's the problem. It's also what happens to them in the course of living their lives. Poverty, violence and loneliness are inherent in a society that puts profits above people, and these are things that drive people crazy.

My rage has given me a great deal of energy and motivation. Still, I've come to the conclusion that bitterness doesn't help me change anything. Demonizing psychiatrists doesn't convince anyone of anything useful. Psychiatrists are not devils, any more than crazy people are. They're not rubbing their hands together, cackling gleefully as they devise new ways to torture people. Even the ones who prescribe massive amounts of drugs and electroshock, I suspect, are almost always convinced that they're doing good. To borrow a phrase from Randy Pritchard, "They have intact delusional systems." I can't do anything about that and I'm not going to waste time trying.

Obviously, it's necessary to keep exposing and fighting psychiatric abuses. But I'm even more interested in discussing and developing better things for people to do than get psychiatric help. Essential to this process is taking a closer look at madness.

Language, belief and experience

Learning about new ways of looking at what's really happening to us when we go mad can make a huge difference to our experience of madness. Imagine, for example, if we could unlearn the idea that anything strange or extremely intense is automatically dangerous and terrifying. Persimmon Blackbridge says,

> When I've flipped out, it's been a really awful experience, but it's hard to separate the experience from how I get treated and my desperate attempts to pass for normal. I'd like to know what my experience would be without all the fear and self-hatred that are so tightly interwoven with it. I'm not saying that if it weren't for all that, it would be a wonderful time. But it would be an entirely different time, I know. And if I could talk about it without constantly looking over my shoulder for the moment when someone's face closes off, and I've gone too far, and they're looking for the door—that would change everything.
>
> The world isn't just *described* by language and by our ideas about it. It's actually *ordered* by those things. Language determines how we catalogue our experiences; what's important to see in the world, and what "doesn't exist," that we shouldn't see in the world. We're taught from a young age how to be in the world and how to experience it. We're not taught how to experience the world while going crazy. It's defined as a bad, ugly, negative situation.
>
> When I was crazy I kept thinking, isn't there someone who knows about how to do this? People keep telling you how to act in order to be normal again. It seems like all the language and ideas are aimed at trying to shut you down.

What you are told about yourself has a huge impact on what you do, and how and who you are. Year upon year of hearing yourself described by a medical label can cause you to see yourself as a walking disease. Being told that you're weak and helpless, if you come to believe it, can make you weak and helpless. Being told that you need expert help can make you need it. Being told that you're bad can make you more likely to do bad things.

Say, for instance, that you have been labelled a psychopath. You are told that unlike other so-called mental illnesses, yours is not only incurable but untreatable. It is drummed into you that you have no conscience. Everyone expects you to behave badly, looks at you as some kind of monster, and misinterprets everything you do. What effect might this have on your behaviour?

Or what if (like most of us) you're diagnosed with a condition that is supposed to be treatable, like "schizophrenia" or "depression"? You're likely to be taught to depend entirely on the psychiatric system, rather than trying to change the situation that brought you into the system. Being told that you are a consumer of mental health services can keep you in that role for life. Your identity is based on consuming those drugs and "services."

And does psychiatry really make it easier to cope? Or does it teach you to see your own thoughts and feelings as symptoms—to fear every emotion? Many "chronic mental patients" choose to end their lives, and the suicides are then attributed to mental illness.

Read the label

I and an increasing number of people I know have chosen the label "crazy." We are often accused of stigmatizing ourselves. But the label "mentally ill" has been used against us by powerful people (psychiatrists, police) to put and keep us in our place: to hospitalize, drug, silence and belittle us. If we're mentally ill, there's something wrong with our minds and we need to be fixed. But if we're crazy, that's not necessarily the case. There is no possible good connotation to mental illness, but it's possible to be dancing like crazy, crazy about something or someone, or crazy happy. Labelling ourselves crazy is an act of defiance. First of all, we do the labelling. But more than that, our label flies in the face of the system. It gives the finger to everyone who has ever told us we're sick.

Labels can be used to put people into tight and uncomfortable boxes, but they can also be stepping stones to liberation. Imagine that you've grown up with people putting you down for not being like them. You are labelled crazy by others and you think you're some kind of alien.

Maybe you have experiences that you don't understand and you're afraid.

One day you act too weirdly, or get too scared, or try to kill yourself, and end up in the hospital. Suddenly, you have a new label: you're a patient. You are liberated from feeling that you're at fault for what's wrong with you and from the terror of having no idea what to do; there are experts you can trust to help you.

Back out in "the community," you're hooked up with a day program or drop-in where a new label awaits you: you're a consumer of mental health services. You are liberated from being the passive recipient of help. You have a group to get involved in. Some things that happened to you inside were lousy, and now you can talk with other consumers and service providers about how to make the system work better.

One day, you meet someone who calls themselves a psychiatric survivor. You talk with them and gradually come to realize that what you've been through in the system has harmed you. You adopt their label. You're liberated from thinking there was something wrong with you in the first place.

You get together with other psychiatric survivors and talk more, and decide that maybe you no longer want to define yourself according to what someone else has done to you. You make room for the idea that the bad things that have happened to you have made you strong and the increasing number of good things in your life are making you even stronger. You are liberated from seeing yourself as "wounded" and from seeing the purpose of your life as "healing" yourself. You're weird, and that's an important and positive part of who you are. You label yourself crazy.

But that's not the end of the story. Craziness is not the only important thing about you. Most people define themselves not according to what they are but according to what they do. You may take on the label "artist" or "housekeeper" or "electrician." At the same time, you may choose to label yourself an activist; you are liberated by deciding that you can act upon the world; you can change things. In the process, you examine and question what's really going on.

Madness

The system teaches that only certain people become "psychotic" under stress, likely because of their genes. But what if it's actually just a matter of how *much* stress you're under? I suspect that anyone who is put in four-point restraints in a little locked room, naked, in the dark will eventually "exhibit psychotic symptoms" no matter how "sane" they may previously have been.

And just what are psychotic symptoms? Have you ever watched a small child having a tantrum—flailing, screaming, striking out? Or have you ever watched a small child who is extremely happy—jumping up and down, spinning around, laughing, shrieking, bouncing off the walls? When adults act like this, it's likely to be seen as a psychotic episode. So is believing or perceiving things the people around you don't believe or perceive—something children also often do.

Again and again, people I've talked to in the movement have talked about how the mental health system, both in hospital and out, treated them like children. Many of us went mad when we were coming into adulthood and our lives were changing too fast. Many of us were put away by our parents. What if many a "schizophrenic" is a young person who is being difficult and has gotten too big to be slapped or sent to his or her room? Once the "diagnosis" is made, someone else can take over doing the slapping (now pharmaceutical rather than "hands on") and the confinement.

The chatter of the very young is dismissed as meaningless, and so is the raving of lunatics. But the *content* of people's madness can have value and meaning, if only symbolic meaning. There is often a grain of truth in even the wildest ideas. For example, people who have been psychiatrized have often had their lives totally controlled and monitored by others, and been given drugs that make it hard to think or care about anything. When you've been subjected to this kind of treatment, thinking that aliens or secret service agents are controlling your brain makes a creepy kind of sense.

Psychiatric staff see the drugs they administer as "settling" their patients. In many cases we were considered "settled" when we felt so horrible we didn't want to move, talk or do anything but sleep. (Of course they noted in our charts that we were withdrawn and lethargic and that these were symptoms of illness.)

What they are trying to settle with the drugs often boils down to emotional, sensory and perceptual changes that tend to be caused by circumstances and events in people's lives. Such changes can also be brought on by hormones, allergies, malnutrition, lack of sleep and many other physical things. (This is important because former psychiatric patients who go into hospital with physical problems are frequently misdiagnosed. A doctor may look at your medical records, find your psychiatric history and dismiss your complaints as being all in your mind. The consequences of this can be disastrous.)

I know people who are positive that psychiatric drugs—or even electroshock—made their craziness (or depression) go away and that the adverse effects are a small price to pay. I can't prove, and am not interested in trying to prove that they're wrong. I believe in any case that much of medicine "works" through the placebo effect; if one trusts the doctor, the pills are often effective. But that doesn't mean that taking them is the best possible thing you can do.

Liberation

It's heavy work, trying to fight brutal injustices that never stop. We in the mad movement (like everyone else) need to find ways to keep our stress levels down. But we need more than that. We need to be free, not only of hospitals and psychiatrists, but of the negative ways in which we've been taught to look at ourselves and of the high value placed on being safe and "normal."

Normality can be a burden. We spend so much energy on not being ourselves, on keeping everything inside, on looking cool. We're supposed to devote our lives to meeting the expectations the world has placed on us: being heterosexual, getting married, having children, being thin, dressing nicely, being "productive," accumulating money and prestige. We're supposed to make do with substitutes for real contact: a handshake, a polite smile, a "how are you" that doesn't really want an answer.

But I believe that the mad movement can take us far beyond that. It has taught me to dream big, to trust big and to take big chances. To dare real closeness and joy and play. I and many of my crazy friends have a great deal to teach people about alternatives, not only to psychiatry, but to other ways in which people are oppressed. We've lived through a lot and we've seen a lot. We've talked and we've thought, and we've helped ourselves and each other and people who are supposed to be sane. We have found ways of living that may not look right to others but that suit us.

With knowledge and experience, we come to power. In celebrating our weirdness and letting ourselves be the strange people we are, we set ourselves free. And with that power and that freedom, surely we can work together to make neuroleptics and electroshock a thing of the past. Surely we can create a thousand things that really work, not for settling people and making them normal, but for relieving them of pain and freeing them to think, feel and do.

BIBLIOGRAPHY

The first thing I'd recommend to anyone interested in finding out more about the international mad movement is *Dendron News*. *Dendron* is the newsletter of Support Coalition International (SCI) and is the hottest movement publication I know of. You can get a sample copy for $3 U.S. by writing to Dendron, P.O. Box 11284, Eugene, OR 97449-3484, USA. You can reach Dendron by e-mail at: dendron@efn.org, or on the World Wide Web at: http://www.efn.org/~dendron/. Support Coalition is an independent nonprofit alliance dedicated to stopping forced psychiatric human rights violations and promoting humane alternatives. SCI is led by psychiatric survivors and its membership is open to all who share its mission.

To check out the *Madness* mailing list, go to their home page at: http://www.io.org/madness/. My web site, the Lunatics' Liberation Front, can be found at http://www.walnet.org/llf/. For a list of back issues of *Phoenix Rising: The Voice of the Psychiatrized*, please write to me at Box 3075, Vancouver, BC V6B 3X6 Canada

And now, the books:

Adams, Patch with Mylander, Maureen. *Gesundheit!: Bringing Good Health to You, the Medical System, and Society through Physician Service, Complementary Therapies, Humor and Joy.* Rochester: Healing Arts Press, 1993.

Alty, Ann and Mason, Tom. *Seclusion and Mental Health: A Break with the Past.* London: Chapman and Hall, 1994.

Arbogast, Doyle. *Wounded Warriors: A Time for Healing.* Omaha, NE: Little Turtle Publications, 1995.

Aronson, Virginia. *Different Minds, Different Voices.* Boca Raton, FL: Cool Hand Communications, 1995.

Barham, Peter. *Closing the Asylum: The Mental Patient in Modern Society.* Toronto: Penguin Books, 1992.

Barham, Peter and Hayward, Robert. *Relocating Madness: From the Mental Patient to the Person.* London: Free Association Books, 1995.

Baur, Susan. *The Dinosaur Man: Tales of Madness and Enchantment from the Back Ward.* New York: HarperCollins Publishers, 1991.

Bayer, Ronald. *Homosexuality and American Psychiatry: The Politics of Diagnosis.* New York: Basic Books, 1981.

Bean, Philip and Mounser, Patricia. *Discharged from Mental Hospitals.* London: Macmillan, in association with Mind Publications, 1992.

Bentall, Richard P., ed. *Reconstructing Schizophrenia.* London; New York: Routledge, 1989.

Billig, Otto and Burton-Bradley, B.G. *The Painted Message.* New Brunswick, NJ: Transaction Publishers, 1978.

Blackbridge, Persimmon. *Sunnybrook: A True Story with Lies.* Vancouver: Press Gang Publishers, 1996.

Blackbridge, Persimmon and Gilhooly, Sheila. *Still Sane.* Vancouver: Press Gang Publishers, 1985.

Bogdan, Robert. *Freak Show: Presenting Human Oddities for Amusement and Profit.* Chicago: University of Chicago Press, 1988.

Boyle, Mary. *Schizophrenia: A Scientific Delusion?* London; New York: Routledge, 1990.

Breggin, Peter R. *Electroshock, Its Brain-Disabling Effects.* New York: Springer, 1979.

–. *Psychiatric Drugs, Hazards to the Brain.* New York: Springer, 1983.

–. *Toxic Psychiatry: Why Therapy, Empathy, and Love Must Replace the Drugs, Electroshock, and Biochemical Theories of the "New Psychiatry."* New York: St. Martin's Press, 1991.

Breggin, Peter R. and Breggin, Ginger Ross. *Talking Back to Prozac: What Doctors Won't Tell You about Today's Most Controversial Drug.* New York: St. Martin's Press, 1994.

–. *The War against Children.* New York: St. Martin's Press, 1994.

Breggin, Peter R. and Stern, Mark, eds. *Psychosocial Approaches to Deeply Disturbed Persons.* Binghamton, NY: The Haworth Press, 1996.

Brown, Phil. *The Transfer of Care: Psychiatric Deinstitutionalization and Its Aftermath.* London: Routledge and Kegan Paul, 1985.

Burstow, Bonnie. *Radical Feminist Therapy: Working in the Context of Violence.* Thousand Oaks, CA: Sage Publications, 1992.

Burstow, Bonnie and Weitz, Don, eds. *Shrink Resistant: The Struggle against Psychiatry in Canada.* Vancouver: New Star Books, 1988.

Bynum, W.F.; Porter, R.; and Shepherd, M., eds. *The Anatomy of Madness: Essays in the History of Psychiatry.* London; New York: Tavistock Publications, 1985, 1988.

Caplan, Paula J. *They Say You're Crazy: How the World's Most Powerful Psychiatrists Decide Who's Normal.* Reading, MA: Addison-Wesley, 1995.

Capponi, Pat. *Upstairs in the Crazy House: The Life of a Psychiatric Survivor.* Toronto: Penguin Books, 1992.

Cardinal, Roger. *Outsider Art.* New York: Praeger Publishers, 1972, 1973.

Castel, Robert. *The Regulation of Madness: Origins of Incarceration in France.* Trans. W.D. Halls. Berkeley: University of California Press, 1988.

Chamberlin, Judi. *On Our Own: Patient Controlled Alternatives to the Mental Health System.* New York: Hawthorn Books, 1978.

Chekhov, Anton. *Ward Six.* Trans. A. Dunnigan. Cutchogue, NY: Buccaneer Books, 1986 (first published in 1892).

Cohen, David. *Forgotten Millions: The Treatment of the Mentally Ill—A Global Perspective.* London; Toronto: Paladin-Grafton, 1988.

Cohen, David, ed. "Challenging the Therapeutic State: Critical Perspectives on Psychiatry and the Mental Health System." Special issues of *The Journal of Mind and Behavior* 11, nos. 3/4, 1990; 15, nos. 1/2, 1994.

Colbert, Ty C. *Broken Brains or Wounded Hearts: What Causes Mental Illness.* Santa Ana, CA: Kevco Publishers, 1996.

Coleman, Lee. *The Reign of Error: Psychiatry, Authority, and the Law.* Boston: Beacon Press, 1984.

Collins, Anne. *In the Sleep Room: The Story of the CIA Brainwashing Experiments in Canada.* Toronto: Lester and Orpen Dennys, 1988.

Copp, Terry and McAndrew, Bill. *Battle Exhaustion: Soldiers and Psychiatrists in the Canadian Army, 1939–1945.* Montreal: McGill/Queen's University Press, 1990.

Digby, Anne. *Madness, Morality, and Medicine: A Study of the York Retreat, 1796–1914.* Cambridge: Cambridge University Press, 1985.

Dinham, Paul S. *You Never Know What They Might Do: Mental Illness in Outport Newfoundland.* St. John's: Institute of Social and Economic Research, Memorial University of Newfoundland, 1977.

Doerner, Klaus. *Madmen and the Bourgeoisie: A Social History of Insanity and Psychiatry.* Trans. J. Neugroschel and J. Steinberg. Oxford: Basil Blackwell Publisher, 1981.

Dols, Michael. *Majnun: The Madman in Medieval Islamic Society.* Oxford: Clarendon Press, 1992.

Donaldson, Kenneth. *Insanity Inside Out*. New York: Crown Publishers, 1976.

Dwyer, Ellen. *Homes for the Mad: Life Inside Two Nineteenth-Century Asylums*. New Brunswick, NJ: Rutgers University Press, 1987.

Ehrenreich, Barbara and English, Deirdre. *For Her Own Good: 150 Years of the Experts' Advice to Women*. Garden City, NY: Anchor Press, 1978.

Epstein, Julia. *Altered Conditions: Disease, Medicine, and Storytelling*. London: Routledge, 1995.

Farber, Seth. *Madness, Heresy, and the Rumor of Angels: The Revolt against the Mental Health System*. Chicago: Open Court, 1993.

Fernando, Suman. *Mental Health, Race and Culture*. New York: St. Martin's Press, 1991.

Fleming, Michael and Manvell, R. *Images of Madness: The Portrayal of Insanity in the Feature Film*. Rutherford, NJ: Farleigh Dickinson University Press, 1985.

Foucault, Michel. *Madness and Civilization: A History of Insanity in the Age of Reason*. Trans. Richard Howard. New York: Vintage Books, 1965, 1973.

Frame, Janet. *Faces in the Water*. New York: George Braziller, 1961.

Frank, K. Portland. *The Anti-Psychiatry Bibliography and Resource Guide*. 2nd ed. Vancouver: Press Gang Publishers, 1979.

Frank, Leonard Roy, ed. *The History of Shock Treatment*. San Francisco: Frank, 1978 (order from Leonard Frank at 2300 Webster St., #603, San Francisco, CA 94115, USA).

–, ed. *Influencing Minds: A Reader in Quotations*. Portland, OR: Feral House, 1995.

Gabbard, Krin and Gabbard, Glen O. *Psychiatry and the Cinema*. Chicago: University of Chicago Press, 1987.

Gallagher, Hugh Gregory. *By Trust Betrayed: Patients, Physicians, and the License to Kill in the Third Reich*. New York: Henry Holt, 1990.

Garton, Stephen. *Medicine and Madness: A Social History of Insanity in New South Wales, 1880–1940*. Randwick, NSW, Australia: University of New South Wales Press, 1988.

Geller, J.L. and Harris, M., eds. *Women of the Asylum: Voices from behind the Walls, 1840–1945*. New York: Anchor Books, 1994.

Gibson, Margaret. *Sweet Poison*. Toronto: HarperCollins, 1993.

Gilboord, Margaret Gibson. *The Butterfly Ward*. Montreal: Oberon Press, 1976.

Gilman, Charlotte Perkins. *The Yellow Wallpaper, and Other Fiction*. New York: Pantheon Books, 1980 (first published in 1892).

Gilman, Sander L. *Difference and Pathology: Stereotypes of Sexuality, Race, and Madness*. Ithaca: Cornell University Press, 1985.

–. *Seeing the Insane*. Omaha, NE: University of Nebraska Press, 1996.

Goffman, Erving. *Asylums: Essays on the Social Situation of Mental Patients and Other Inmates*. Garden City, NY: Doubleday, 1961.

–. *Stigma: Notes on the Management of Spoiled Identity*. Englewood Cliffs, NJ: Prentice-Hall, 1963.

Golden, Stephanie. *The Women Outside: Meanings and Myths of Homelessness*. Berkeley: University of California Press, 1992.

Gordon, Barbara. *I'm Dancing As Fast As I Can*. New York: Harper and Row, 1979.

Gordon, Felicia. *The Integral Feminist: Madeleine Pelletier, 1874–1939*. Minneapolis: University of Minnesota Press, 1991.

Gotkin, Janet and Gotkin, Paul. *Too Much Anger, Too Many Tears: A Personal Triumph over Psychiatry.* New York: New York Times, 1975; HarperPerennial, 1992.

Grobe, Jeanine, ed. *Beyond Bedlam: Contemporary Women Psychiatric Survivors Speak Out.* Chicago: Third Side Press, 1996.

Gruen, Arno. *The Insanity of Normality: Realism as Sickness: Toward Understanding Human Destructiveness.* Trans. H. and H. Hannum. New York: Grove Weidenfeld, 1992.

Hill, David. *The Politics of Schizophrenia: Psychiatric Oppression in the United States.* Lanham, MD: University Press of America, 1983.

Hirsch, Sherry; Adams, J.K.; and Frank, L.R., eds. *Madness Network News Reader.* San Francisco: Leonard Roy Frank, 1974 (booklet — order from Leonard Frank at 2300 Webster St., #603, San Francisco, CA 94115, USA).

Horwitz, Elinor Lander. *Madness, Magic, and Medicine: The Treatment and Mistreatment of the Mentally Ill.* Philadelphia: Lippincott, 1977.

Hughes, John S., ed. *The Letters of a Victorian Madwoman.* Columbia, SC: University of South Carolina Press, 1993.

Hyde, Christopher. *Abuse of Trust: The Career of Dr. James Tyhurst.* Vancouver: Douglas and McIntyre, 1991.

Illich, Ivan. *Disabling Professions.* Salem, NH: M. Boyars, 1977.

Ingleby, David, ed. *Critical Psychiatry: The Politics of Mental Health.* Harmondsworth: Penguin Books, 1981.

Jodelet, Denise. *Madness and Social Representations: Living with the Mad in One French Community.* Trans. T. Pownall, ed. G. Duveen. Berkeley: University of California Press, 1992.

Johnson, Ann. *Out of Bedlam: The Truth about Deinstitutionalization.* New York: Basic Books, 1990.

Jones, Colin and Porter, Roy, eds. *Reassessing Foucault: Power, Medicine and the Body.* London: Routledge, 1994.

Kakar, Sudhir. *Shamans, Mystics and Doctors: A Psychological Inquiry into India and Its Healing Traditions.* New York: Alfred A. Knopf, 1982; Chicago: University of Chicago Press, 1991.

Kaysen, Susanna. *Girl, Interrupted.* New York: Turtle Bay Books, 1993.

Kesey, Ken. *One Flew Over the Cuckoo's Nest.* New York: New American Library, 1962.

Kirk, Stuart A. and Kutchins, Herb. *The Selling of DSM: The Rhetoric of Science in Psychiatry.* New York: A. de Gruyter, 1992.

Kiss Me You Mad Fool: A Collection of Writing from Parkdale Activity and Recreation Centre. Toronto: Positive Print, 1991.

Kitzinger, Celia and Perkins, Rachel. *Changing Our Minds: Lesbian Feminism and Psychology.* New York: New York University Press, 1993.

Kleinman, Arthur. *Rethinking Psychiatry: From Cultural Category to Personal Experience.* New York: The Free Press, 1988.

–. *Social Origins of Disease: Depression, Neurasthenia, and Pain in Modern China.* New Haven, CT: Yale University Press, 1986.

Kleinman, Arthur and Lin, T.-Y., eds. *Normal and Abnormal Behaviour in Chinese Culture.* Dordrecht, Holland: D. Reidel Publishing, 1980.

Laing, R.D. *The Politics of Experience.* New York: Pantheon, 1967.

Laing, R.D. and Esterson, A. *Sanity, Madness and the Family: Families of Schizophrenics.* New York: Basic Books, 1971 (first published in 1964).

Landrine, Hope. *The Politics of Madness.* New York: Peter Lang Publishing, 1992.

Lapon, Lenny. *Mass Murderers in White Coats: Psychiatric Genocide in Nazi Germany and the United States.* Springfield, MA: Psychiatric Genocide Research Institute, 1986.

Leonard, Linda Schierse. *Meeting the Madwoman: An Inner Challenge for Feminine Spirit.* New York: Bantam, 1993.

Lessing, Doris. *The Four-Gated City.* New York: Knopf, 1969.

Littlewood, Roland and Lipsedge, Maurice. *Aliens and Alienists: Ethnic Minorities and Psychiatry.* New York: Routledge, Chapman and Hall, 1989.

Lunebeck, Elizabeth. *The Psychiatric Persuasion: Knowledge, Gender, and Power in Modern America.* Princeton: Princeton University Press, 1994.

MacKenzie, Charlotte. *Psychiatry for the Rich: A History of Ticehurst Private Asylum, 1792–1917.* London: Routledge, 1993.

Majzels, Robert. *Hellman's Scrapbook: A Novel.* Dunvegan, ON: Cormorant Books, 1992.

Masson, Jeffrey Moussaieff. *Against Therapy: Emotional Tyranny and the Myth of Psychological Healing.* New York: Atheneum, 1988.

Massumi, Brian. *A User's Guide to Capitalism and Schizophrenia: Deviations from Delueza and Guattari.* Cambridge: MIT Press, 1992.

McKague, Carla and Savage, Harvey. *Mental Health Law in Canada.* Toronto: Butterworths, 1987.

McLaren, Angus. *Our Own Master Race: Eugenics in Canada, 1885–1945.* Toronto: McClelland & Stewart, 1990.

Mental Patients Association. *Madness Unmasked.* Vancouver: Mental Patients Publishing Project, 1974.

Micale, Mark S. and Porter, R. *Discovering the History of Psychiatry.* Oxford: Oxford University Press, 1994.

Millett, Kate. *The Loony Bin Trip.* New York: Simon and Schuster, 1990.

Mitchinson, Wendy. *The Nature of Their Bodies: Women and Their Doctors in Victorian Canada.* Toronto: University of Toronto Press, 1991.

Modrow, John. *How to Become a Schizophrenic: The Case against Biological Psychiatry.* Everett, WA: Apollyon Press, 1995.

Monroe, Russell R. *Creative Brainstorms: The Relationship Between Madness and Genius.* New York: Irvington Publishers, 1992.

Morgan, Robert F., ed. *Iatrogenics in Professional Practice and Education: When Helping Hurts.* Billings, MT: Morgan Foundation Publishers: International Published Innovations, 1994.

Morgan, Robert F.; Roueche, B.; Freidberg, J.; Breggin, P.; and Frank, L.R., eds. *Electroshock Treatment over Four Decades: The Case Against.* Billings, MT: Morgan Foundation Publishers: International Published Innovations, 1994.

Nahem, Joseph. *Psychology and Psychiatry Today: A Marxist View.* Ann Arbor: Books on Demand, 1981.

Newman, Fred. *The Myth of Psychology.* Greenwich, NY: Castillo International, 1991.

Ng, Vivien W. *Madness in Late Imperial China: From Illness to Deviance.* Norman, OK: University of Oklahoma Press, 1990.

Nisker, Wes "Scoop." *Crazy Wisdom*. Berkeley: Ten Speed Press, 1990.

Noel, Barbara with Watterson, Kathryn. *You Must Be Dreaming*. New York: Poseidon Press, 1992.

Payer, Lynn. *Disease-Mongers: How Doctors, Drug Companies and Insurers Are Making You Feel Sick*. New York: John Wiley, 1992.

Peterson, Dale, ed. *A Mad People's History of Madness*. Pittsburgh: University of Pittsburgh Press, 1982.

Piercy, Marge. *Woman on the Edge of Time*. New York: Knopf, 1976.

Pilgrim, David and Rogers, Anne. *A Sociology of Mental Health and Illness*. Bristol, PA: Taylor and Francis, 1993.

Plath, Sylvia. *The Bell Jar*. London: Faber and Faber, 1967.

Porter, Roy. *Mind-Forg'd Manacles: A History of Madness in England from the Restoration to the Regency*. London: Athlone Press, 1987.

–. *A Social History of Madness: The World through the Eyes of the Insane*. London: Weidenfeld and Nicholson, 1987, 1988.

Proctor, Robert N. *Racial Hygiene: Medicine under the Nazis*. Cambridge: Harvard University Press, 1988.

Rabinowitz, Max. *The Day They Scrambled My Brains at The Funny Factory*. New York: Zebra Books, 1978.

Rack, Philip. *Race, Culture and Mental Disorder*. New York: Tavistock Publications, 1982.

Ralph, Diana. *Work and Madness: The Rise of Community Psychiatry*. Montreal: Black Rose Books, 1983.

Richman, David et. al. *Dr. Caligari's Guide to Psychiatric Drugs*. San Francisco: Leonard Roy Frank, 1984 (booklet—order from Leonard Frank at 2300 Webster St., #603, San Francisco, CA 94115, USA).

Ripa, Yannick. *Women and Madness: The Incarceration of Women in Nineteenth-Century France*. Trans. C. Menage. Cambridge: Polity Press, 1990.

Robitscher, Jonas. *The Powers of Psychiatry*. Boston: Houghton Mifflin, 1980.

Roccatagliata, Guiseppe. *A History of Ancient Psychiatry*. New York: Greenwood Press, 1986.

Rogers, Anne; Pilgrim, David; and Lacey, Ron. *Experiencing Psychiatry: Users' Views of Services*. London: Macmillan in association with Mind Publications, 1993.

Rosenberg, Charles and Golden, Janet, eds. *Framing Disease: Studies in Cultural History*. New Brunswick, NJ: Rutgers University Press, 1992.

Rosenberg, Morris. *The Unread Mind: Unraveling the Mystery of Madness*. New York: Lexington Books, 1992.

Rothman, David. J. *Conscience and Convenience: The Asylum and Its Alternatives in Progressive America*. Boston: Little, Brown, 1980.

Sapinsley, Barbara. *The Private War of Mrs. Packard*. New York: Paragon House, 1991.

Sass, Louis A. *Madness and Modernism: Insanity in the Light of Modern Art, Literature, and Thought*. New York: Basic Books, 1992.

Scull, Andrew. *Decarceration: Community Treatment and the Deviant: A Radical View*. Englewood Cliffs, NJ: Prentice-Hall, 1977.

–. *Madhouses, Mad-doctors, and Madmen: The Social History of Psychiatry in the Victorian Era.* Philadephia: University of Pennsylvania Press, 1981.

–. *Museums of Madness: The Social Organization of Insanity in Nineteenth-Century England.* Harmondworth: Penguin Books, 1979.

–. *Social Order/Mental Disorder: Anglo-American Psychiatry in Historical Perspective.* Berkeley: University of California Press, 1989.

Sexton, Anne. *To Bedlam and Partway Back.* Boston: Houghton-Mifflin, 1960.

Sharkey, Joe. *Bedlam: Greed, Profiteering, and Fraud in a Mental Health System Gone Crazy.* New York: St. Martin's Press, 1994.

Sheehan, Susan. *Is There No Place on Earth for Me?* Boston: Houghton Mifflin, 1982.

Shortt, S.E. *Victorian Lunacy: Richard M. Bucke and the Practice of Late Nineteenth-Century Psychiatry.* Cambridge: Cambridge University Press, 1986.

Showalter, Elaine. *The Female Malady: Women, Madness and English Culture, 1830–1980.* New York: Pantheon Books, 1985.

Shutts, David. *Lobotomy: Resort to the Knife.* New York: Van Nostrand Reinhold, 1982.

Siebert, Al. *Peaking Out: How My Mind Broke Free from the Delusions in Psychiatry.* Portland, OR: Practical Psychology Press, 1995.

Simmons, Harvey G. *From Asylum to Welfare.* Downsview, ON: National Institute on Mental Retardation, 1982.

–. *Unbalanced: Mental Health Policy in Ontario, 1930–1988.* Toronto: Wall and Thompson, 1990.

Simon, Bennett. *Mind and Madness in Ancient Greece: The Classical Roots of Modern Psychiatry.* Ithaca: Cornell University Press, 1978.

Spence, Jonathan. *The Question of Hu.* New York: Knopf, 1988.

St-Amand, Neré. *The Politics of Madness.* Trans. E. Garmaise and R. Chodos. Halifax: Formac Publishing, 1987.

Still, Arthur and Velody, Irving, eds. *Rewriting the History of Madness: Studies in Foucault's "Histoire de la folie."* London: Routledge, 1992.

Supeene, Shelagh Lynne. *As for The Sky, Falling: A Critical Look at Psychiatry and Suffering.* Toronto: Second Story Press, 1990.

Susko, Michael, ed. *Cry of the Invisible: Writings from the Homeless and Survivors of Psychiatric Hospitals.* Baltimore: Conservatory Press, 1991.

Szasz, Thomas. *The Age of Madness: The History of Involuntary Mental Hospitalization.* New York: J. Aronson, 1974.

–. *Ceremonial Chemistry: The Ritual Persecution of Drugs, Addicts, and Pushers.* Holmes Beach, FL: Learning Publications, 1985.

–. *Cruel Compassion: Psychiatric Control of Society's Unwanted.* New York: Wiley, 1994.

–. *Ideology and Insanity: Essays on the Psychiatric Dehumanization of Man.* New York: M. Boyars, 1983 (first published in 1970).

–. *Insanity: The Idea and Its Consequences.* New York: Wiley, 1987.

–. *Law, Liberty and Psychiatry: An Inquiry into the Social Uses of Mental Health Practices.* New York: Macmillan, 1963.

–. *A Lexicon of Lunacy: Metaphoric Malady, Moral Responsibility, and Psychiatry.* New Brunswick,

NJ: Transaction Publishers, 1992.

–. *Schizophrenia: The Sacred Symbol of Psychiatry.* New York: Basic Books, 1976.

–. *The Manufacture of Madness: A Comparative Study of the Inquisition and the Mental Health Movement.* New York: Harper and Row, 1970.

–. *The Myth of Mental Illness: Foundations of a Theory of Personal Conduct.* New York: Harper and Row, 1974.

–. *The Myth of Psychotherapy: Mental Healing as Religion, Rhetoric, and Repression.* Garden City, NY: Anchor Press/Doubleday, 1978.

Tenenbein, Silva. "Paradigm Lost/Paradigm Regained: The Second Coming of Dissociation." Master's thesis, Simon Fraser University, Vancouver, 1995.

Thomas, Gordon. *Journey into Madness: The True Story of Secret CIA Mind Control and Medical Abuse.* New York: Bantam Books, 1989.

Trent, James W. *Inventing the Feeble Minded: A History of Mental Retardation in the United States.* Berkeley: University of California Press, 1994.

Tuormaa, Tuula E. *An Alternative to Psychiatry.* Sussex, UK: The Book Guild, 1991.

Ussher, Jane. *Women's Madness: Misogyny or Mental Illness?* Amherst, MA: University of Massachusetts Press, 1992.

Valenstein, Elliot S. *Great and Desperate Cures: The Rise and Decline of Psychosurgery and Other Radical Treatments for Mental Illness.* New York: Basic Books, 1986.

Vice, Janet. *From Patients to Persons: The Psychiatric Critiques of Thomas Szasz, Peter Sedgewick and R.D. Laing.* New York: Peter Lang Publishing, 1992.

Ward, Mary Jane. *The Snake Pit.* New York: Random House, 1946.

Warsh, Cheryl Krasnick. *Moments of Unreason: The Practice of Canadian Psychiatry and the Homewood Retreat, 1883–1923.* Montreal: McGill; and Kingston: Queen's University Press, 1989.

Weeks, David and James, Jamie. *Eccentrics: A Study of Sanity and Strangeness.* London: Weidenfeld and Nicholson, 1995.

Weinstein, Harvey. *A Father, a Son and the CIA.* Toronto: J. Lorimer, 1988.

Weiss, Peter. *The Persecution and Assassination of Jean-Paul Marat As Performed by the Inmates of the Asylum of Charenton under the Direction of the Marquis De Sade.* Trans. G. Skelton and A. Mitchell. New York: Atheneum, 1966.

Weisskopf-Joelson, Edith. *Father, Have I Kept My Promise? Madness as Seen from Within.* West Lafayette, IN: Purdue University Press, 1988.

What's Wrong with the Mental Health System (order from Rational Island Publishers, PO Box 2081, Main Office Station, Seattle, WA 98111, USA).

Witkiewicz, Stanislaw Ignacy. *The Madman and the Nun, and Other Plays.* Seattle: University of Washington Press, 1968.

Wolinsky, Howard and Brune, Tom. *The Serpent on the Staff: The Unhealthy Politics of the American Medical Association.* New York: G.P. Putnam's Sons, 1994.

Wood, Mary Elene. *The Writing on the Wall: Women's Autobiography and the Asylum.* Urbana: University of Illinois Press, 1994.

Woodson, Marle. *Behind the Door of Delusion.* Niwot, CO: University Press of Colorado, 1994 (first published in 1932).